THE
PERFECT ROOM

ROCKPORT

THE
PERFECT ROOM

GLOUCESTER MASSACHUSETTS

ROCKPORT PUBLISHERS

PROFESSIONAL SECRETS FOR FLAWLESS STYLE

SARAH LYNCH

PIP NORRIS

First published in the United States of America
by Rockport Publishers, Inc.
33 Commercial Street
Gloucester, Massachusetts 01930-5089
Telephone:: (978) 282-9590
Facsimile: (978) 283-2742
www.rockpub.com

10 9 8 7 6 5 4 3 2 1

The Perfect Dinning Room, The Perfect Kitchen, The Perfect Bedroom, and The Perfect Open Plan by Sarah Lynch.
The Perfect Living Room, The Perfect Bathroom, and The Perfect Outdoor Room by Pip Norris.
Perfect Legends of Design by Regina Cole.

Cover and Book Design: Stoltze Design
Layout and Production: Heath O'Leary
Cover Photograph: Photo Disc/Mel Curtis, Photographer
Back Flap Photograph: Jeremy Samuelson
Back Cover Photograph, left: Grey Crawford/Beate Works
Back Cover Photograph, middle & right: Jeremy Samuelson

Printed in China

CONTENTS

INTRODUCTION

In learning how professionals and homeowners realize their "perfect home," you can easily make your home perfect—a place where you can lead your private everyday life, as well as the public life that encompasses the people you love, your friends, and your professional life.

Webster tells us that perfect is "Freedom from fault or defect. Satisfying all requirements." That is a good goal for life and the environments we live in. To think of perfection in the sense of absence of what we don't want and the satisfaction of what we do want, helps reduce the stress of creating our own perfection.

COMBINE COMMON SENSE WITH ELEVATED STYLE.

This book will be invaluable to answering the "why" of design, not just how to copy others. It covers lots of bases, in a range of styles. Creating your perfect home can seem like an overwhelming project. *The Perfect Room* breaks apart this daunting task into smaller more easily accomplishable pieces.

How many times have you picked up an interior design book or magazine only to be more confused? The publication may be full of beautiful pictures, of beautiful rooms, but it also lacks the information to allow you to achieve your desires for your rooms. When preparing to write this intro, I found the book systematically answering the same questions, and addressing the same fears that my clients have when they are working on their homes.

In *The Perfect Room*, the authors show how others have addressed the same issues that you are faced with. It is also a source of inspiration.

As I counsel my design clients, you should first do some soul searching. How do you want to feel in your rooms? How do you want others to feel when they are in your home? What are your rooms to be used for? Answer these simple questions, roll up your sleeves, get out your note pad and start dreaming up your idea of your perfect home. You are now armed with more than paint chips from the hardware story and pretty pictures.

You can achieve the perfect expression of your life within the walls of the place you call home.

Good luck with your project and dreams. And most of all, remember to have fun!

Gregor D. Cann
Designer/Writer

Call attention to the interior space with pure white, as seen here in a long room dominated by a mantle at one end. Notice how smooth white finishes with black accents are at once lively and restful, and the blocky pieces provide ample sitting space and mimic the overall proportions of the room.

WHAT IS A PERFECT LIVING ROOM?

It's one that you find beautiful, comfortable, and useful. There is not one perfect style, or floor plan, or color scheme that is the ideal. If the room is a textbook beauty but does not suit your taste or lifestyle, it is not the perfect room for you. But whatever the style or type of living room you want, the basics are the same: proportion and balance, color and light.

PROPORTION · BALANCE · COLOR · LIGHT

The perfect living room, the real ideal, has good bones, meaning quality construction materials, architectural detail, and agreeable proportions—a pleasing relationship of length to width to height. If your room is beautiful, even when empty, your job will be less complicated. When decorating rooms such as this, sometimes all you need to do is highlight what is already there. If, for example, your room has large windows overlooking a beautiful landscape, it may need only comfortable seating. A stately room in a time-honored building with crown moldings and high ceilings might benefit simply from a traditional décor. Rooms that are not perfect from the outset are more of a challenge. These rooms might have some wonderful qualities but will greatly benefit from tricks—optical illusions and diversionary tactics—to make them true beauties.

Use optical illusion to create a sense of proportion in odd spaces: Place large pieces of furniture against windowed walls or alcoves to balance their weight with outdoor vistas. Balance dark wood with the glow of color: Here the chair and a glowing color palette soften the piano. A filigreed string of ornaments draws the eye and subtly unifies the windowed space.

PROPORTION

Without proportion, even rooms with beautiful furnishings just don't come together. Good proportion is often the underlying factor that makes rooms pictured in the stylish magazines work so well: Imperfect proportion is what makes it so hard to bring the look into your own home. The secret is this: In less than ideal spaces, use optical illusion to give the impression of good proportion.

Jennifer Post, a New York designer, is masterful at bringing stylish sophistication to banal spaces. She creates deliciously chic apartments out of less than perfect spaces by creating synergy between rooms. She helps the architecture when necessary, raising door heights and opening passages to create vistas from foyer to living room. But without going to the expense of construction (or destruction) she can create an interesting space with a favorite decorating tactic–lots of tempered glass and mirrors. The effect on the viewer is dramatic–when you walk into a room, your eye keeps moving. Post gives distinction to the mundane with simple techniques–she gives the space the starring role.

BALANCE

Wherever you use it, balance can be the glue that holds a stylish room together. Take cues from the approach of Architect Michael Graves, who is noted for his sense of balance; he often employs symmetry or creates it where it is needed. To give a room a "centered" quality, Graves places a fireplace or windows opposite a doorway to create a sense of proportion where none previously existed.

HOW TO GET THE LOOK: GETTING WHITE RIGHT

"All white" is the easiest design style to make your own. Whether painted, glazed, whitewashed, draped, or upholstered, you can keep a subtle range of colors in your rooms by using different tints of white. Here are some easy rules to follow to get the mix right:

Painting With White Use a single paint finish (either eggshell or semi-gloss) on ceiling, walls, and trim. Keep in mind that "white" includes a bevy of shades extending from bright white to ivory to beige; interior designers like to choose a warmer shade for walls, while reserving cooler, brighter whites for the ceilings and moldings. Be sure to test first, because white walls reflect the color of the furniture and floors. Save the pure whites for upholstery.

White Accessories Designer and antique dealer Jim Lord has other tips for decorating with white (besides his humorous caveat—"don't have children!") that involve accessories. "Texture adds warmth to white," says Jim. Tactile materials such as sisal, wicker, concrete, gesso, fabric, and old painted wood keep the self-contained color scheme from looking unapproachable.

^ Anchor all-white interiors with graphic simplicity—a sweep of dark floor and polished accent table.

^ Reflect architectural details like the decorative molding, fireplace, and shelving seen here with clean square lines—the upholstered pieces and the shape of the rug. The quiet colors and simple shapes strengthen the beauty of the space.

< Let a clean look take the starring role if your room has no outstanding architectural elements. Crisp white walls and slipcovers, upholstery and linear ebony tables mimic the simple beauty of the black and white photographs mounted to define a sitting area.

< Add a dash of color in the throw pillows or accessories to enliven the space and help link it visually to any adjacent rooms that can be glimpsed through the doorways.

THE PERFECT CONTEMPORARY LIVING ROOM

You admire the appearance of the perfect contemporary room you see in the design magazines. You love the look but can't quite get it right in your own home? Let's deconstruct this fine example, looking at all its elements and how they work together to create this perfect contemporary look.

COLOR The color palette in this room is a contemporary favorite—graphic black and white. But, it's not that simple. There are several whites in the room adding warmth and depth, which make the room both more interesting to look at and a more welcoming space. The largest walls are the warmest shade; the fireplace wall is a lighter, but still soft shade; the sofa and chair yet another; and the ceiling and moldings the brightest white. Not only are the shades different, the textures are also varied. Different textures absorb or reflect light differently, altering our perception of the color. White fabric will absorb more light than glossy white paint. The fabric will appear more muted.

FURNITURE The furniture and accessories are predominantly linear pieces with square corners. The suede and leather mix of the black chair highlights the shape of the cushions, adding dimension to what could appear as a black cube. The backless settee in off-white upholstery opens up the configuration so the room feels larger, and one is not faced with the back of a sofa upon entering the room. The seating is arranged for small gatherings and intimate conversation, with the fireplace as focal point. The pieces are set at right angles to each other so that the configuration taken as a whole mimics the form of each piece, which reinforces the graphic quality of the entire room.

FLOORING Light wood flooring is left bare for a swept-clean look, but a graphic area rug is added for warmth and definition of the sitting area. Its earthy tones work to ground the furniture in the room linking the natural wood floor to the black and white elements.

ACCESSORIES Most obvious accessories are within the palette. The bank of black and white photos, framed and matted also in black and white, is hung in a roughly rectangular grouping in keeping with the proportions of the room and furnishings. But here the décor takes a personal turn with the introduction of humor in the portraits. And the painting over the fireplace is whimsical, but remains strictly within the design parameters of the décor, keeping the overall look cohesive.

BALANCE While straight lines and right angles dominate this décor, some curves are included for balance. The side-table with its curvilinear pedestal base and generally airy appearance softens the dense, blocky forms of the other furnishings. And a touch of apple green, actually green apples, and a green cachepot for the lone potted plant, also act as a balancing element for the black and white palette.

Each piece has been carefully selected, the light and proportion of the room taken into consideration, and the personality of the owners revealed—the perfect contemporary living room is then realized.

^ Frame mismatched pictures identically
to create the illusion of a matched set.

Tie a room together using color schemes as a tool, as has been done with the russet hues in this living room. You can easily produce a harmonious whole and a pleasant feeling of constancy without needing to get too intense or obvious about it. This is also a good way to successfully marry contemporary details with antique furniture, as has been done to great effect here.

COLOR

Color changes the appearance of a room dramatically, so consider this issue very carefully when addressing your living room. Remember that tonality essentially derives from the three primary colors—red, yellow, and blue. To put it most simply, all other colors are simply a blend of these three. Using the purity of the primary colors will result in very dominant spaces, so more often than not the subtler secondary and tertiary colors are employed in a multitude of hues. Do think about employing a primary color, however, as a focal point. Nothing will define the presence or a shape of something as well.

Use color to create optical illusions throughout the home. If you have low ceilings then consider painting them with a satin or gloss finish, which will reflect light and, therefore, help to visually heighten the ceiling, thus enhancing the sense of space and light. If your room has somewhat uneven proportions consider visually smoothing these out by painting the entire room in one color—i.e. skirting boards, walls, window frames—the lot. Remember also that the color scheme will need to complement your furniture.

Combine color and texture for visual interest: Here, a tactile mix of fabrics brings a monochromatic scheme forward. Beige suede, beige linen, and glossy beige ceramic look like three quite different hues on each surface. Consider picking out more versions of the same color in objects such as artwork and lamps.

< Use pure colors to draw attention to your favorite furnishings, as has been done here with this vivid chair. Try to create a sense of balance by picking out the same color in another feature of the room, as has been cleverly done with the floral arrangement and by matching the chair fabric to the color detail in the draperies.

Red and yellow are warm colors and tend to draw your room inward, creating a more cozy and intimate space. Cooler colors—such as blue and green—do the opposite and can be employed in a room to make it appear more spacious. Try painting a large color patch on your wall before committing to it. The larger, the better, for you will get a much clearer idea of the impact. You'll be amazed just how different slight variations of a shade can look.

Experiment with surface textures to affect the color. A trick to remember is that a shiny surface reflects light and a matt surface absorbs it. Be aware of this and mix textures to add another dimension to your room.

One effective way of combining the benefits of a neutral, light-enhancing color with the exuberance of a bolder, richer one is to paint a feature wall. You will get a wonderful splash of color in your room without letting it overpower and drown out the contents.

A color scheme within the palette of natural materials provides a hushed backdrop for beautiful wood tones and sculptural furnishings.

PERFECT LIVING ROOM PALETTES

In the 1960s, David Hicks, the London decorator who devised a purple and magenta living room for cosmetics impresario Helena Rubinstein, said: "Of all the many raw materials at the designer's disposal, color is the most exciting and rewarding—and the most dangerous."

SOFT The color palette of the living room will have a powerful effect on how one feels in the room. Neutral colors and soft tones of blue and green are more restful than other palettes—a good choice if your living room is where you kick off your shoes and relax at the end of the day.

BRIGHT Bright colors and reds and yellows invigorate, which works well in a room geared to entertaining and lively conversation. Deep rich tones of greens and browns can create a sedate, peaceful aura for a room for quiet reflection. Choosing the mood you want is a good starting place for color selection, but it's just the beginning.

LIGHT The amount of natural light is as important to consider as the room's purpose. While generally speaking, the more natural light your room gets, the more saturated colors it will tolerate. Yet, a poorly lit room can be quite elegant done in saturated colors. The sure-fire method for getting the right effect is to paint a large test swatch and check it at different times of day, to see how it changes as the sun moves across the sky.

SIZE Also take into consideration the size of the room. Bold and dark colors are said to "advance" seemingly closing in a space, while lighter colors recede, making a room feel larger. While "advancing colors" sounds ominous, sometimes a small room gets added warmth and coziness from a bold treatment that makes it seem even smaller than it is. A tiny powder room, for example, can become an elegant spot for guests to freshen up in luxury when painted in a deep lacquered red and accented with black accessories.

COLOR KEYS Architect Jorge Trelles, who works in Miami, advises that the key to adding color to a house is to stay within the palette of its natural surroundings. "The trick," he says, "lies in muting or brightening the hues to suit the natural light—a tropical palette should be several octaves lower where the sun is less intense."

Color can also be a brilliant solution to both extremes of architectural difficulties. Overwhelming blandness can be totally obliterated with a sweep of deep color on the walls. Overly ornate architecture can be neutralized by blending of trim and wall color, or by averting the eye with a colorful diversion.

> Deep rich tones make for a peaceful, tranquil atmosphere.

A room does not need to be perfectly symmetrical to project a balanced look. But in a room that is symmetrical except for one anomaly, you need to disguise the anomaly or the room will always feel off kilter. Add a folding screen to one corner, as seen here, to offset the single post in the opposite corner. An upholstered partition centered between the two corners will keep the eye focused on the middle of the span where linear furnishings and artwork will impose further order while providing an inviting resting spot.

ARTWORK

There are some formulas for hanging artwork that always seems to work. A pair of pictures—similar in feeling, such as two opera posters—will coexist happily side-by-side. It is best to frame them identically so that they appear to be a matched set, or, if the pictures differ in size but nevertheless look good together, hang them one on top of the other (the smaller one goes on top). Groupings of three are always satisfying to the eye—if the space is narrow, group the pictures in a stack. Try lining pictures up in a row, allowing one or two inches between. Groupings of four (especially botanical prints or photographs) make a stunning arrangement hung two over two, as illustrated on page 15.

Peter Carlson, a Los Angeles interior designer, favors rectangular groupings that are almost architectural in layout. "Position the pictures," he advises, "on the floor first." Get the perimeter straight, and then fill in the middle of the arrangement. "Anchor the corners," Carlson says, "and split pairs of pictures to balance the top or bottom corners." If no pairs are available, create unity by anchoring the corners with images matted with dark mats. "They carry more weight than light mats," says the designer. Focus next on the center of the layout. "Something small with a very wide mat gives the eye a place to land," says Carlson. "So, too, will one large picture, or two or three related pieces." It's not necessary to achieve a perfectly symmetrical grid. Once the perimeter is straight, remaining frames don't need to align.

HOW TO GET THE LOOK:
LEAVING WINDOWS BARE

In large open rooms, with no walls to obscure the sun streaming in through the windows, the best approach can sometimes be to leave the windows bare.

Create Drama Floor-to-ceiling windows take on the dramatic status of a major architectural element when they are left unadorned, and can give a room a muscular, industrial atmosphere.

Add Props If this approach is simply too naked for your taste, consider bare windows modified by an ever-changing array of paintings and photographs on the windowsills. A large mirror placed against a wall or propped on a mantel will capitalize even more on the available light, with both sun and views adding extra dimension to the room.

Evening Strategy Add discreet blinds or roll-up shades that can be unfurled after the sun goes down, to cure the "black-hole" effect of bare windows that lack an illuminated view. To keep them from distracting from the architecture of the windows during the day, conceal the blinds or shades in a recessed pocket deep in the sill or above the window for roll-down blinds.

‹ Windows left unadorned bring drama to the rest of the room.

LIGHT   Careful consideration of your natural light source is crucial in planning·"the perfect living room." Understand the natural light source completely, not just when it enters but where, at what angle, and for how long. In any room you should never underestimate how important maximizing natural light is. This is particularly important in a living room for this is generally where you spend much of your time, be it eating, relaxing, or entertaining.

You won't always want direct sunlight. You may well want diffused light, so consider curtains that are to some degree transparent, as seen here. Use them to adjust the light flow. Also try to keep the windows clean, as this will make a surprising difference to the clarity and strength of your natural light source.

Use a mirror as a light-enhancing device. See here how it helps throw daylight around this calm, cream-colored sitting room, thus increasing the light levels. The shiny parquet floor also reflects rather than absorbs light, adding to the bright, airy nature of this room. Think laterally about window coverings—try installing louvered shutters as in this photo, instead of curtains.

You will need to have some sort of command over the natural light entering your home. Filter it according to the time of day and time of year, for its intensity varies greatly. Bearing this in mind, louvered shutters are fantastic window coverings. They enable complete control of the light flow; you can fold them away for a totally obstruction-free view and unhindered flow of light or you can adjust the louvers according to the angle of the sun, creating soft filtered bars of light.

Natural light will either be a room's greatest asset, or a lack thereof, its greatest downfall. Bear this in mind when thinking about how you can best utilize this crucial design tool.

Always stop to consider the visual balance of your room, for you may unconsciously destroy this if you don't. If an architectural equilibrium already exists (note the windows in this photo), then mirror this elsewhere, as has been done here with the dual armchairs, vessels, and pictures. You can thus easily create a continuously successful balance within your room.

MORE LIGHT

Sometimes by replacing a window with another only a few centimeters larger, or even by simply repositioning it, you can enhance a room's light beyond expectations. Consider, if need be, the ways in which you can add extra natural light to your living area. Is a skylight appropriate? Is its installation a realistic option? If not, could you perhaps add a low-slung strip of windows at floor level to draw in more light or maybe draw it through from another room by using frosted glass for the dividing wall?

HOW TO GET THE LOOK: ARRANGING FURNITURE

"Think," said the late Mark Hampton, "of rooms in which conversation can flourish...in which visitors feel immediately at home and would rather sit than stand...." Rooms like this, advised the great decorator, are ones where the furniture is arranged well. "They appear to be comfortable to the eye even before one has experienced the physical comfort."

Use Focal Points The location of the room's focal point—a fireplace, a view, a fabulous rug—determines how much seating you can get into a room. Large spaces may accommodate two seating areas—one grouping of sofa and flanking chairs in front of the fireplace, and another grouping at the other end of the living room.

Be Realistic Know how you really intend to use the room and decorate it accordingly. Inveterate party givers will want to have comfortable furniture above all else—plus movable chairs and plenty of ottomans for impromptu conversations. If your living room is the place everyone gathers to watch football games, then by all means keep the television there—just be sure to disguise it behind cabinet doors.

‹ Give a sitting area its own presence, even in an open floor plan. While here the bank of doors leading out to the patio is a strong focal point, emphasized by the contrasting blue paint, equally alluring is the high-backed banquette sofa upholstered in a plush fabric of quieter tone and nestled into the corner. The brightly colored throw pillows draw the eye to that space. But it is the artwork hung off center and surprisingly toward the doors that serves to define the area, creating a boundary by stopping the eye before it wanders to the doors beside them.

Shiny surfaces, such as high gloss paint, mirrors, glass, and chrome, are the perfect materials for a versatile dining area. Separate a dining space within a great room by positioning lighting overhead that feels appropriate, like hanging pendant lamps or an ornate chandelier with a matching center arrangement on the table, just below it.

WHAT MAKES THE PERFECT DINING ROOM?

Contrary to popular belief, the perfect dining room is not an amalgamation of all your Sunday best including the heirloom Chippendale furnishings and your finest china on display. Now that the days of nightly (or even weekly) family sit-down dinners seem to have faded into black and white, there is a need to redefine the modern dining room.

ELEGANCE · VERSATILITY · DRAMA · LAYERING

Nowadays, a dining room can be a place where breakfast is taken, calls are made, and work is done. The more versatile the design, the more purposes the dining room can have: home office, library, entertaining, you name it. But, what sets this room apart from any other multi-purpose room is that sense of special occasion that is synonymous with dining room—elegant details like collectible accessories and stylishly matched furnishings are what make this room a place that can quickly be gussied up for dinner at eight. The finishing flourish is, as always, a matter of preference, but the fact is dining rooms have traditionally been the place where a heavy dose of drama is agreeable because such a limited amount of time is spent there. Rich colors, theatrical lighting, bold floral arrangements, and large paintings all work so easily in a dining room.

ELEGANCE   "A perfect dining room is one that doesn't feel like it's waiting for an event to happen,"
says New York designer Vicente Wolf. His tips for countering that sense of static include
using mixed-matched chairs around a table so that it feels more like a sitting area in which
you dine than a space strictly for dining. Perfectly ordered place settings and identical
chairs lined up at a table can make a dining room feel like a banquet hall rather than a res-
idence. Another suggestion of Wolf's is placing a softly upholstered banquette against the
wall for a comfortable place to sit; then, when it's time for a meal, you can pull the table
up to the banquette—just make sure that the seat level matches the other chairs.

Adding unexpected elements to a dining room is the best way to create an elegant setting
for entertaining. Instead of the usual—table and chairs with a matching sideboard and
china cabinet—try adding a unique side table or étagère. Display collectibles, whether it is
a painting, sculpture, or exotic antique such as an elephant-shaped birdcage. Potted plants
and tall trees add a fresh dose of life and are an easy way to create vertical lines in a room
with mostly horizontal planes.

Wolf's trademark style is one of easy elegance and for dining rooms his use of fabrics
and accessories translates beautifully. He suggests upholstering the walls or hanging panels
of fabric in order to quiet the clinking noise of silver and glass. There are so many hard
surfaces in dining rooms, he says, that layering the walls with loose hanging fabric and
paintings will soften the noise. Here, iridescent silk works like a curtain to reveal one painting
and acts as a backdrop for another oversized painting. Wall sconces and standing lamps
are placed against the fabric as an added layer. The result is a dramatic room that feels
elegant and yet versatile enough to sit around for a leisurely breakfast.

< This dining room, designed by Vicente Wolf, defies tradition by layering one elegant detail upon another. White upholstered side chairs are mixed with 1940s armchairs around a traditional dining table. Surrounding the table, unexpected details like side tables and pendant lamps occupy corners while a curtain of dressy silk lines the walls and acts as a theatrical curtain for oversized original paintings.

THE PERFECT DINING ROOM SETTING

The function of a dining room is, essentially, to impress. Unlike bedrooms, kitchens, and living rooms, a dining room does not have to perform. Kitchens must be work-friendly, bedrooms should be restful, but a dining room can simply be the room where you show off your style without worrying too much about functionality.

STYLE A highly versatile dining room that can double as a home office or play area is a practical idea but don't sacrifice the identity of your dining room. It's the one room where it's perfectly acceptable to go over the top with high style or dramatic design.

ATMOSPHERE A dining table and chairs are essential but apart from these, you can furnish your dining room with anything you like. A curvaceous chaise in the corner can impart the feeling of a Dionysian feast; potted palm trees, ornate goblets, and wall tapestries will add to the setting. As any event planner will advise, atmosphere is everything.

PROPS Furnishings and architecture are important as always, but props can work wonders to make a room entertainment-ready. Fresh-cut flowers, floating in bowls at each place setting or a bold centerpiece, are a must. And dramatic lighting is essential; unless you have a fabulous chandelier, forget overhead lights that can feel imposing. Instead try using wall sconces along with tabletop candles.

PERFECT DETAILS In the rooms seen here, a collection of Regency chairs, eclectic china patterns, and other neoclassical details come together for an incredible two-room dining experience. The formal dining room, with the round table, feels like it was lifted out of nineteenth-century France with topiaries marking the garden entrance, a chandelier dripping with crystals—all in an elegant palette of muted yellow and beige. The next room takes a bolder approach by converting a desk into a dining table and setting it on an angle in a room chock-full of details. This room has fewer architectural elements, so the drama must come from the furnishings and accessories—a hanging Japanese screen, leopard-printed bench, and an assortment of plates and ceramics create a theatrical setting for dining room overflow.

^ A detail from the informal dining area shows an intricate sideboard covered in a collection of creamware. This would be a fancy element fit for a more formal room were it not for the bench upholstered in a leopard print pulled up to it and the Japanese paneled scene that hangs behind. A propped corner like this adds infinite drama to an already eclectic dining area.

> Just off the formal dining room, this less structured room uses furnishings rather than architecture to show off its dramatic style. The theme of pineapples and palm fronds lend their informal essence to a collector's paradise, full of plates and ceramics and Regency chairs.

< A French neoclassical dining room is staged for an elegant breakfast *al fresco*. With manicured topiaries marking the door to the garden, notice that this room has meticulous details down to the plaster frieze on the wall to the upholstery on the chairs to the silver candlesticks.

VERSATILITY

A well-designed dining room is a place where you want to retreat, a place where you can sit and enjoy a candlelit meal and after-dinner conversation or even just a quiet place to sit and relax. Remember that it can also be a great place to spread out a work project or do homework. A dining room should be inviting and practicle and yet, still special.

A versatile dining room is a necessity in this densely populated world. Who has the space for a breakfast nook, a kitchen table—*and* a formal dining room? Dining rooms will become obsolete along with parlors and dressing rooms unless we make them amenable to our modern needs. Make the room work, not just for meals but also for lounging or even as an art studio. Consider some of the new convertible designs on the market, like a small square table that flips open and folds out to seat sixteen (and all without those pesky removable leaves).

NIGHT Recessed spotlights overhead pour on the drama at night. Dinner for eight is sleek and modern and the added reflections on the chrome and glass impart a formality. The lighting makes the entire table a centerpiece that feels ready for a party.

DAY A sleek monochromatic dining area in a modern loft is perfect for any meal. The cool gray palette in the carpeting and on the chairs is matched with glass and chrome for a minimal look. Color is added with a Japanese painting and floral centerpiece, but the overall effect is still pure, simple, and quiet.

A wall of windows make this lofty space feel more like an atrium than a formal dining room. A collection of antique chairs and colored glass add to the sense of a lush exotic dining experience. At night, with dozens of candles lit, the effect is entirely different but equally dramatic. An elephant-shaped birdcage adds to the Far Eastern atmosphere.

TRANSFORMATIONS

Think of your dining table simply as a surface and the edicts of dining room design will begin to fall away. Who says it has to be a finely polished wood table? Why not a slab of colored Corian over a sawhorse base or a glass top over a sculptured pedestal? The point is that the more unconventional your dining room is, the more purposes it can serve. Less formal materials such as glass, chrome, and plastic work equally well as shiny mahogany and teak wood and they make the room feel infinitely less stuffy.

For family dining rooms that transform to seat eighteen, try incorporating folding furniture. The types that are out there aren't just banquet quality to be kept in the basement and promptly covered with a giant tablecloth. Modern chairs that stack easily or tables that can unfold to three times their size are perfect for a convertible dining area. If materials like painted metal or plastic seem a little too informal for holiday time, they can easily be slip covered in any fabric—consider an awning stripe for added color or a sheer-flowing white for an dreamy dining experience.

> Let stunning architectural elements, such as the vaulted ceiling and arched doorway seen here, act as decoration for your dining room. Here, the less formal glass-topped table and classic chairs add to the elegance and drama.

PERFECT FARMHOUSE STYLE

Farmhouse style might be the ideal answer to a versatile dining area—warm, informal, simple yet quaint. A rough-hewn plank table, spindle back chairs, and a Shaker-style chandelier are perfect for casual meals in what still feels like a true dining room. Although farmhouse style has different regional looks and can span several centuries, the overall effect bridges all of these—an easy atmosphere without fuss or fancy but with brightly colored accents and a homemade flavor.

Quintessentially casual and yet perfectly elegant, this colorful dining room has all the right pieces. An enamel topped table takes center stage while carved cathedral-backed chairs follow suit. (For more guests, pull up the painted bench.) The painted glass-front cupboards showcase a pottery collection and stand out against sage-green walls.

Place spindle-backed chairs around a classic plank table for an easy Shaker-style dining room. Simple lines and lots of natural wood are basic elements of farmhouse style. Built-in shelves, wide-plank floorboards, and a stenciled boarder complete the look.

Classic Spanish details like the rubbed plaster walls and blackened steel chandelier make this Mediterranean farmhouse dining room feel cozy. Informally arranged with a butcher-block table, painted bench, and metal chairs, this room can be quickly converted from a prep station into a dining room.

TIME-WORN TEXTURES A wrought-iron chandelier, open-hearth fireplace, wide-plank table, and a time-worn hutch—this is the recipe for a perfect farmhouse dining room. It doesn't matter what type of architecture your house has to acquire this look; exposed ceiling beams and bead board wainscoting are helpful but not necessary. If you are lucky enough to start from scratch, try stenciling a border at the ceiling or chair rail height in order to jumpstart the farmhouse look. An oval braided rug or any colorful open weave on the floor will add color and warmth.

RUSTIC FINISHES When choosing a dining table, don't limit your options to the traditional farmhouse wooden table. There are also dark stained versions with brass fittings and enamel-topped variations that feel equally rustic. Dining chairs can be anything from spindle-back chairs to carved shapely side chairs painted in a range of country hues: lemon yellow, forget-me-not blue, or a creamy white. Try using a tall-backed bench like a deacon's seat, painted in a contrasting color, in lieu of a couple chairs for a quaint, mismatched look.

COUNTRY COMPLEMENTS For accessories, Depression glass and milk glass are the perfect complement to farmhouse style. Stenciling on anything from chairs to bookcases to standing tray tables will also add a homespun, vintage look. Sweetly patterned cotton fabric or lace works for a window valance but a bold check or bright stripe would also fit right in. Finally, fresh flowers are a must: big wild sunflowers overflowing from a Fiestaware pitcher are the perfect centerpiece on a farmhouse dining table.

HOW TO GET THE LOOK: USING RED

Red is a powerful color for any room. It is dramatic and daring. It's also a very warm, nurturing color that is said to promote conversation and increase the appetite.

Formal or Informal Dining rooms have a tradition in red, especially formal dining areas dressed in rich garnet and deep scarlet. But red can also work hard for a modern dining room by standing out against clean lines and spare shapes—it can often be the element of drama in an informal dining area.

Welcome Flattery Red is the perfect color for a dining room because it is so inviting, says San Francisco designer, Jeffry Weisman, "especially at night. And it makes everyone look great." When red is lit only by candles, it takes on a warm and welcoming glow. In Weisman's classically elegant dining room (right) red walls bring the room together. A polished dining table and chairs with apricot-colored cushions and a hand-painted silk chandelier are more dramatic and stylish when set against crimson walls.

Jeffry Weisman's elegant take on a dining room marries all the elements of gustatory comfort: soft pillows to sit on, a warm rug underfoot, a centerpiece of roses, dim lighting from a silk chandelier, and flickering candlelight. This large traditional dining table could feel very formal and rigid were it not for the deep crimson stroke of drama and the personal touch of the roses, the rug, and the painting.

DRAMA

"Since you spend limited amounts of time in a dining room, you can take the intensity of color and not tire of it quickly," San Francisco designer Jeffry Weisman says. The dining room is the place to take your style to the hilt with wild, saturated color and lots of it. Don't forget to consider the ceiling as a canvas for color; it will help make the ceiling feel lower—a boon for a room where guests are usually seated. Lowering the ceiling height and sensing the reflection of candles on a warmly hued ceiling can make the whole room feel infinitely cozier.

Apart from the classic red, consider deep chocolate browns and rich aubergine for an elegant dining room. Wedgwood blue is another classic color that sets off many china patterns and goes beautifully with gold or silver accents. Accenting the dining table with items that highlight the major design elements is the quickest way to finish off the look. To bring out the beauty of a rich wall color, use as many reflective surfaces as possible: mirrors, silver, gold, and candles to make all of these sparkle. Sleek gold candlesticks and gilded picture frames work beautifully against warm color schemes such as reds, deep oranges, and golden yellows, while silver accents work best in cooler color palettes such as deep blues and greens. Since the majority of flatware comes in silver, it is fine to mix and match the metals in a dining room, with say a silver-plated butler service and gilt mirrors on the walls.

< To separate a dining space from a large living area, try using color to demarcate the borders. Here a rich, classic shade of red acts a room divider along with a Turkish rug that serves as an island for the dining table. When using dramatic color, it is not necessary to pair it with ornate designs. A simple table and chairs works like a charm for this contemporary dining area.

LAYERING

Formal dining rooms, if you have the space and the need for them, can pose several design challenges. The room should have enough drama and style to be the perfect setting for entertaining guests on special occasions but it shouldn't feel as though it were anticipating the event. Like a diamond necklace that just waits in the jewelry box to be worn, fancy dining rooms can look lonely and out of place on a regular Wednesday.

The best way to give a formal space some life is to add layers of soft textures and some sort of organic element such as a plant or a bowl of fresh fruit or even a birdcage. Layering the walls with fabric adds a sense of movement and fluidity. Thriving plants make the room feel vibrant. And natural textures such as linen, raw silk, or natural coir or sisal rugs ground the room and bring it back to everyday reality.

As many dining rooms don't have windows, the best way to bring light in is to fake it. In this dining room London designer and maestro of softening walls Kelly Hoppen hung panels of white against chocolate brown; the result feels either like a columned outdoor room or like a circle of windows surrounding the table. A natural wood table and sisal rug make the room feel naturally light and airy despite its dark exposure. If you do have a window, no matter how small, always take advantage of the miracle of mirrors. During the day, the reflection of light will make the most rigid dining room feel airy and light. At night, the mirror will reflect twinkling candles and glittering silver.

Consider using a bright yellow or warm apricot on the walls to mimic morning sunshine during the day. If you are married to the concept of neutrals, try designing wall hangings or arranging paintings so that they give the impression of large windows. A giant pastoral painting on one wall with a mirror just opposite can make a room feel larger and open to the world outside, even if it is stuck smack in the middle of a colonial house.

> Located in a corner of an apartment, this formal dining area must make the most of a tight squeeze. A mirror hung adjacent to the only window opens the space up and doubles the amount of light coming in. Softening the classical hard qualities of fine dining, upholstered slipper chairs and sheer window fabrics make the space feel cozy yet elegant.

A rectangular table in a room the same shape, with a parade of identical chairs lined up like soldiers, can sometimes feel static and posed. Here, London designer Kelly Hoppen makes use of fabric panels on the walls to emphasize the geometry of the room while softening it at the same time. It is a structured room but hardly rigid with the addition of soft fabrics and natural elements like the potted plants and sisal rug.

Notice that this sleek minimal loft is divided into "rooms" simply by the arrangement of furniture. The dining area is its one space, confined by a kind of strict organization that keeps it cohesive: The identical chairs match the illuminated shoji screen wall, the design of the table and chairs matches the low, spare lines of the rest of the furniture but the color palette is warmer and more contrasting than the living area.

PERFECT ASIAN MINIMALISM

The latest trend in home design, style that takes its cue from Eastern aesthetics, tends to be more stripped down and pure than overly ornate or detailed designs. It is a logical reaction to intricate, highly decorated styles, and the association with serenity and clearing the mind is what makes these Asian influences so appealing. The combination of sleek lines, spare furnishings, a neutral, muted palette, and a series of repeated shapes creates an atmosphere that feels exotic and restful.

ORGANIZATION This works perfectly for a dining room, where form and function must meet and be harmonious. The key to this look is organization and storage. We tend to have way too much stuff and a dining room can feel ruled by the storage of china, candles, tablecloths, and glassware. For a clean, minimal aesthetic we must learn to organize our stuff and put it away, out of sight so that the clutter of everyday life doesn't hinder our relaxation.

A natural color palette is one of the tenets of Asian style. Here the floors are painted black and the dark wood table is stained in a coffee-colored stain. The chairs are upholstered in a shade of wheat that matches the natural bamboo wall. Heavy pieces are countered with tall skinny candles and the heft of the table is balanced by the cutouts in the chairs.

HIDDEN STORAGE The design of this kind of home sanctuary involves much forethought. For a dining room, built-in storage seems to be the primary element. Celeste Cooper, whose signature aesthetic is sleek and spare, likes to have floor-to-ceiling china and crystal closets as part of wall paneling or upholstered walls. When closed, the storage units become invisible as part of the walls, but open a panel and you have instant access to everything you need. Shoji screens are another great way to hide clutter and replace it with an even series of panels that add to the simple geometry of a room.

REPETITION With this style, repetition feels right at home. A line of identical chairs, evenly spaced along a clean-lined table, is the perfect dining situation. Candles, spaced at equal distances along the table, work well, although a cluster of rocks or tall, skinny candles can make a dramatic statement in such an organized atmosphere. Candlelight or recessed lighting are natural ways to illuminate an Asian dining room. Walls or screens, lit from behind, make a dramatic wall treatment and add interest without disrupting the serenity.

Effortlessly combine kitchen, dining area, and living room in an open plan design. A slick kitchen counter with tripod stools acts as a dining table and enhances the airiness of the architecture. Track lighting that floods the walls of the kitchen, serves as a room divider by separating the kitchen with a glowing border. A concrete floor and white brick wall help unify the space with an industrial uniform that is warmed by velvety pillows on the sofa and art hung on the wall.

WHAT MAKES THE PERFECT

The conversion of warehouse buildings into lofty apartments has changed the face of city living into something chic yet industrial and altogether alternative. In fact, open plan apartments are now so desirable that many newly constructed buildings are being designed without dividing walls and practically stripped bare of architectural ornament. Now that loft living has become an urban norm, making a comfortable home out of wide-open spaces is a common decorating dilemma.

ARRANGEMENT · SCALE · SPACE

The problem is moving into an empty box with limitless possibilities for the placement of furniture, fixtures, and artwork. With so much space, it would be easy for these apartments to feel sterile and too industrial. The best way to create a cozy atmosphere out of large open spaces is to divide the space into traditional-type "rooms" by arranging furniture, lighting, and floor treatments. The key is not to feel like you have to use up all the space as you would a normal, compartmentalized floor plan. The beauty of open plan architecture is the drama of scale: oversized windows, high ceilings, and a broad expanse of uniform floors. Highlight these features with light pieces of furniture that act as a foil to the huge room; but use them sparingly—make open space part of your design.

ARRANGEMENT　If your open space is reserved for living and dining areas only, there are endless design choices that will work. These two areas can easily blend into each other and share many of the same features. If possible, private spaces like bathrooms and bedrooms should be cordoned off into their own separate areas. This allows the freedom to design an open living space that doesn't call for privacy screens or window shades to block out daylight. Instead, a living/dining/cooking area can be an integrated living area that shares spaces for sitting, eating, and preparing food.

SCALE　No matter how you arrange your living spaces or rooms be sure to use airy furnishings that won't break up the space with their heft. A glass table on skinny rolling legs and tripod bar stools is much less imposing than a sturdy kitchen island with a butcher block top, and this design makes the kitchen feel much more tied to the rest of the room. Low-lying furnishings will also make high ceilings and tall arched windows feel like a cathedral. Lighting is another important element for open-plan rooms. Since there isn't a controlled area to illuminate, designated spaces must be lit with either overhead spotlights or carefully placed task lighting.

Use several different elements to define a sitting area within the open plan. An area rug creates the primary border of the room with a low coffee table as the centerpiece. Surrounding the walls of the room are low seats and cushions that emphasize the height of the ceiling and windows—a giant painting on the wall plays up this game of scale.

The kitchen sets itself apart with a colorful tiled backsplash and curved black counter. The unfortunate trick to having an open plan room is that you can't close the door on a messy or cluttered room. For kitchens that are incorporated into the rest of the apartment, the aesthetic must match the rest of the space. In this case, this means a well-organized storage system and matching modern stools.

SPACE Deciding how to divide space when not given any parameters can be tricky. First, consider natural light when drawing the imaginary lines. If you have a square apartment with one wall of windows, dividing it into quadrants using room dividers might not be the best idea even if it does seem the most logical. Instead, try using spatial borders with the arrangement of furniture or lighting to define the "rooms." Rugs, of any shape or size, are also a good way to carve out a "room" within your one giant living space.

Once you have defined the borders of function areas, treat them like any room with walls. Task lighting should be placed where it is needed, at eye level. When you don't have to consider doorways and windows, arranging furniture can be much more imaginative. Place sculpture and standing lamps in the corners to help close in the room and make it feel more secure. Or simply, rotate the entire arrangement so that it feels slightly off-the-grid and infinitely more interesting.

< Stylistically, the apartment feels completely uniform with clean white walls, track lighting, and new wood flooring. And yet, you still feel as though you are moving from room to room as you travel to different elevations and in and out of different floods of light. For a tiny, one-room apartment, dividing the space with built-in levels and loft beds is the best way to break up the space and maintain a sense of openness.

^ With one wall occupied entirely by built-in bookcases, a well-divided space still feels cohesive. On the lower level a classic dining table is personalized by this library wall and on a raised platform, a study can be closed off with sliding sections of wall.

If possible, the easiest way to create rooms within one wide-open space is to place them on different levels. In the apartment seen here, a book-lined space is diligently divided with the use of stepped up levels and sliding walls. Track lighting overhead helps to further define the space so that one-room living feels organized and spacious. The use of simple, modern design and classic furnishings in a light color palette clarify an already clear-cut floor plan.

Polished and sleek, this kitchen makes the most of its space but doesn't attempt to cram it all in. Using reflective surfaces and smooth wood finishes, it feels bigger than it is and its sleek design is unobtrusive but declares itself a professional kitchen without apology.

WHAT MAKES THE PERFECT
KITCHEN?

The perfect kitchen is the perfect example of personal opinion. Some people want
a well-organized laboratory for their culinary experiments; others want room for
friends and family to gather while they cook; and still others prefer the clutter of
a kitchen full of gadgets and a collection of loved dishes and pots. The common
thread, however, is that a kitchen should be fully functional and customized for
the cook who will use it.

FIXTURES · ACCESSORIES · LAYOUT · MATERIALS

The perfect kitchen has a few technical details in common, like a host of professional cooking
gear including a convection oven, a Subzero refrigerator, and a Dacor cook top. How about
infinite counter space and countless shelves of hidden storage? What cook doesn't want fresh
produce? Imagine an herb and vegetable garden just outside a pair of French glass doors. But
apart from these dreamy kitchen details, the rest is up to personal style.

Whether you prefer impenetrable marble for a prep station or a time-worn wood counter, the
type of materials chosen for a kitchen will determine the aesthetic. The difference between stainless steel and polished wood cabinetry is great when it is used as the primary material in the
space. For kitchens, where all the necessary elements must fit together like a puzzle, little room
is left over for personal effects and style statements. The style must be in the design, so plan your
kitchen carefully and consider how you want it to work and how you want it to feel.

FIXTURES

If you have the space and the budget, bring your dream kitchen to life for an ideal cooking experience. If starting from scratch, consider making the kitchen the center of the home (where it was traditionally placed before the concept of hired help pushed it behind a more presentable dining room). More and more, kitchens are becoming a gathering place for families and not just while meals are prepared but simply because they are the most inviting room in the home. The kitchen, now outfitted with telephones, televisions, and computers, offers snacks, entertainment, and overall comfort.

Of course, a dream kitchen should not only be spacious and comfortable, but allow a culinary expert to easily create just about anything. This means that there should be a state-of-the-art cook top; regular and convection ovens; dozens of cubic refrigeration space; and professional-strength ventilation. Not all of this may be necessary but it can't hurt if creating a fantasy kitchen.

The most common amenity of all dream kitchens is space. The room to move about freely or enough open space to accommodate several cooks is essential to a comfortable kitchen. Seemingly infinite storage options, all within easy reach, is another key element. But the number one request made to kitchen designers is the need for counter space. Built-in islands are a good way to add counter space in a kitchen; if islands are large enough they can act as a prep station or even house necessities such as a stove or under-counter storage.

> Notice how the lofted ceiling in this Arts and Crafts-style kitchen allows for a wall of glass-fronted cabinets that are as unassuming as a support beam. Windows both below and above the cabinets make it feel as though you are cooking in a tree house while working at any point along the long counter. Uniform cherry wood paneling throughout this kitchen (including the front of the appliances) combine with the well-planned workstations for a complete dream kitchen.

< A more classic example of a cook's fantasy, this kitchen combines old-fashioned style with modern-day amenities. Butcher-block counter surfaces, a hanging pot rack, bead board painted white, and glass-fronted cabinets all are classic elements of a country kitchen. But state-of-the-art Viking appliances and a cook top located on a spacious center island are subtle reminders that this kitchen, bathed in sunlight, is a "right-now" design.

> Hard surfaces can be warmed by a series of recessed lighting, as seen here, to add a soft glow to this elevated kitchen. With an island prep station that also acts as an eating area, the view out the window is offered to everyone. Cathedral arched cabinets and classical architecture make this hi-tech kitchen feel homey and unobtrusive.

This light-filled kitchen feels like a virtual herb garden with a selection of potted herbs and plants adding a healthy dose of life. Exposed ceiling beams and a personalized collection of antique furnishings and displayed china and cookware transform this into the perfect country kitchen. The clean white Corian counters and new fittings are made warm and welcoming with lots of natural wood elements.

THE PERFECT COUNTRY KITCHEN

Country kitchens seem to never go out of style. Even in the most modern homes, the kitchen is associated with fresh foods and slow-cooked aromas. Classic themes of fruits, vegetables, antique collectibles, and copper pots are right at home in a kitchen that strives to be welcoming and comforting. Even if your kitchen is fully fitted with the most modern appliances on the market, you can still create a "country" look with just the right style statements.

FARM FRESH The number one ingredient for a country kitchen is GREEN. There should be plants in all kitchens as a way to impart a sense of freshness but country kitchens work harder to bring the outdoors in. Fruits and vegetables can be stored in hanging baskets or simply line a windowsill to ripen. If you have big windows, don't cover them with blinds; instead, frame them with sheer drapes or none at all. The country kitchen is a haven for home cooking and farm-fresh ingredients. For year-round reminders of this, consider wallpaper, fabrics, or antiques that illustrate fruits, vegetables, or other garden varieties like chicken wire to reinforce cabinet fronts.

SIMPLE MATERIALS Country kitchens take advantage of a few simple materials: wood, tile, enamelware, all in a natural color palette. An abundance of warm wood tones makes a country kitchen complete. A smooth patina on wideboard wood floors and farmhouse plank tables can be emphasized with a thick butcher-block island top or vintage pieces with a worn, golden tone. Natural wood is the original kitchen material, and although it is not indestructible (it needs to be oiled and cared for to prevent water damage), it feels clean and fresh against painted wood cabinets, white enamel appliances, and even newer materials like stainless and Corian.

^ Consider a green kitchen with natural stone counters to bring the outdoors in. The leafy color on the walls and cabinetry is the perfect backdrop for white pottery, fresh flowers, and a spectacular view. This corner becomes a lookout perch high atop the mountains.

In this carefully constructed kitchen, a center island provides much-need counter space and added shelving with open cubbies in the base. For a nice collection of dishes and cookware, open shelving is the perfect marriage of storage and style. Cabinets and drawers in a cream-colored paneling that also stretches across the appliances is a nice way to keep a kitchen looking organized.

ACCESSORIES

Accessories and collectibles rule the style of kitchens. Unlike other rooms where you can choose fabrics, shapes, and sizes, kitchens offer less freedom for expression of style. After fitting in all the necessary elements, the only question left is what to display. Artwork aside, a kitchen can turn accessorizing into smart storage options. Cute enamelware canisters are an old-fashioned way to keep sugar, flour, and salt; a collection of china can be shown off in open shelving or even hung on the walls. Copper pots can be hung alongside professional-strength versions, from a wall-mounted pot rack or a wrought-iron hanging pot rack. The trick is to make your storage choices look like a personal style statement, so take care to hide the blackened pots and chipped dishes out of sight.

Choosing cabinetry is the equivalent of picking out a fabric for major upholstery. It needs to be functional; don't choose a style that easily shows fingerprints or is difficult to open and close. Combine attractive style with easy-to-use knobs or pulls. If you have an organized shelving system, glass-fronted cabinets are a good choice; there are old-fashioned options or more modern variations on see-through cabinets that allow finding what you need to be a quick, easy task. Open shelving and cubbies are a bright idea for displaying stylish pots and bowls or even for showing off a collection of teapots or glassware. For pantry areas and stuff that is not as aesthetically pleasing, use matching cabinets with solid fronts rather than glass, or the mish-mash of labels and boxes can feel like clutter.

> A combination of glass-fronted cabinets, standard drawers, and lower cabinets allow for a variety of storage options. Attractive dishes and glassware can be stored above while pots, pans, and the standard jumble of cooking wares can be hidden below. Stacking plates on a dining table or buffet is another organized way of showing off attractive dishes.

LAYOUT

When you have a limited amount of space to work with and delusions of a grand fantasy kitchen, you have to plan very carefully. Boston designer Cheryl Katz refers to this type of kitchen as "a machine or a tight ship that makes every inch of space count." In her own town-house home, Cheryl and her design partner and husband, Jeffery, painstakingly carved a pristine kitchen out of a 9-foot by 9-foot (2.7 meter by 2.7 meter) space.

In these cases, you must consider the best appliances and configurations for taking advantage of a limited amount of space. For instance, you may love a domed Gaggenau stainless hood but in a teeny kitchen, you may have to settle for something more space-conscious. As for other dream appliances, weigh your priorities. If you must have a doublewide refrigerator but rarely make anything but salads with all these perishables, consider buying a compact range to make room for your fantasy fridge. With so many household goods on the market that perform double-duty, now is the time to consider the new technology ovens that perform as regular and microwave oven all at once. They may be a little bit pricier but the space saved will make using it so much simpler.

< In small spaces, the best way to make up for a cramped feeling is to cover the whole assemblage in one flat color. In this case pale butter yellow, from floor to ceiling, gives the impression of light, airy space. Turning a standard kitchen design ninety degrees, makes the best use of this galley-shaped kitchen and breaks it into separate work stations.

^ Tucked into a corner, this square station houses a stove top as well as an oven. The clever design allows the two appliances to face different directions so that the oven does not open directly under the stove. It also maintains the view from the corner window that lets light in through open, steel shelving into the rest of the kitchen.

The same space-saving techniques go for storage and seating areas, too. A drop-leaf table or counter top is one of the smartest ideas for a small kitchen. Lift it up for a breakfast bar for two or as extra counter space for chopping vegetables. Rolling carts are another option for additional counter and storage space that can be rolled out of the way when too many cooks are in the kitchen; these are now available in a variety of configurations including ones with cutting surfaces and pot racks built in.

> ‹ This sink area also works as a
> counter space and prep area.
> Standard overhead cabinets
> are painted the same color as
> the walls and additional,
> open shelves were added in
> front of windows so that the
> architecture of the room is
> not interrupted and it feels
> larger and looks brighter.

FITTED OR UNFITTED?

After living for years in her well-designed—tight ship—kitchen, Cheryl Katz and her family out-grew the 9-foot-by-9 foot (2.7 meter by 2.7 meter) space. So they took over the ground floor of their townhouse, which already had a sink, and began assembling a huge working kitchen, piece by piece.

Once a refrigerator and stove were set up, the rest of the pieces were added here and there, as needed. A stainless steel worktable was brought in from a restaurant supply company to act as a center island and became a favorite homework station for Katz's two children. Open shelving was created from steel brackets found at Home Depot and 1/2-inch glass shelves. Steel lockers act as cabinets and pantry. "All of the pieces are unfitted (not built-in) and it's so much more versatile that it puts our perfectly fitted kitchen to shame," says Katz.

"A kitchen doesn't need to be a well-oiled machine," she adds. "Think of it the way you do any other room. It's just an assemblage of the right type of pieces for their function."

HOW TO GET THE LOOK:
KITCHENETTES THAT WORK

Turning a space reserved for something else into a kitchen is not an easy task. And making the most of the tiny kitchenette that a studio apartment was blessed with feels nearly impossible. However, there are ways to overcome awkward kitchen designs.

Designed Many of the poky little overpriced apartments in downtown Manhattan still have bathtubs in the middle of their kitchens but ingenious designers make the most of such defects by laying a thick slab of wood over a defunct bathtub and covering it with a tablecloth to make a quick kitchen table.

Unconfined If your small kitchen area is unworkable, don't confine it to its designated space. Add storage and utility elements in the next room or around the corner for added workspace. This galley kitchen was fitted snugly into a strip of room but not all the elements could squeeze into the space. Rather than trying to cram in all the appliances, the refrigerator is on the opposite wall, giving more space to the sleek design and display area.

Polished This polished wood and stainless steel kitchen area puts its best face forward with a cleverly constructed open plan that takes up very little space but doesn't seem apologetic for being there. It's a smart, elegant, and useful corner of the living room.

^ Making dinner at twilight never seemed so neat. This well-organized kitchen requires a short stride to the fridge but makes cooking convenient and easy with sleek cabinets and various levels of shelving.

< In one-room apartments or small living spaces, big kitchens are not always a priority. This narrow kitchen island designates a small sliver of living space to the kitchen and leaves it open so that no sunlight is sacrificed.

THE PERFECT MODERN KITCHEN

A modern kitchen feels like a racecar. Sleek, aerodynamic and sexy, modern style is about transforming classic forms into memorably graphic shapes, textures, and colors. When it comes to kitchens, designers and architects seem to want to push the envelope of modern, using new materials in innovative ways.

UNADORNED Kitchens are essentially about work so design should focus on the most practical aspects: function, safety, and durability. Modern style does not add ornament in an effort to hide this fact. Instead it deconstructs the "decorated" parts of design and leaves the construction bare. Steel girders and I-beams are revealed to be admired, poured concrete flooring is left bare, cement pavers are exposed for a modern take on wall treatments. In short, a modern kitchen is a machine where we can see all the moving parts.

EFFICIENT Los Angeles-based architectural designer, Brian Murphy, is known for his slick and colorful kitchens. "Everyone is kind of quirky when it comes to kitchens," says Murphy. "One client needs to have a pizza oven, another needs room to entertain, another would prefer a sofa since she doesn't cook at all. But knowing how a kitchen will be used dictates the design." Murphy favors tight, efficient spaces that function as more than just a kitchen. "You need to consider the hang-out coefficient," he adds. Extra space that simply serves as walk-through areas should be considered for separate functions within the kitchen. A well-lit nook can serve as a prep station and also a painting studio.

EDITED The final element of a modern kitchen is that it must be kept clutter-free. Unlike country kitchens or vintage filled kitschy rooms, a graphic modern design requires a true sense of organization. Put away collectibles and tchotchkes, in favor of one bold bowl of fruit or a giant mural lit by a spot light. Modern style is about clean lines and fashionable restraint.

< Display dishes in frosted glass cabinets rather than translucent glass and the effect will feel sleeker and more modern.

^ Notice that the architectural elements here are left exposed to be admired and poured concrete flooring is left bare, for a modern take on kitchen design.

< A curved wall of natural wood is the defining characteristic of this stunning kitchen. Acting as a hood for the entire cooking space, it arches over a rectilinear island with a black marble top and takes some of the rigidness out of this hard-working kitchen. A study in opposites, the warm cream paint disarms the cold, slick stainless steel, and the black elements are in stark contrast to the warm wood floors.

THE PERFECT KITCHEN
65

MATERIALS

Stainless steel is a favorite material for modern kitchens. It's clean and industrial yet shiny and elegant. Professional quality appliances and restaurant supplies started the trend in stainless steel, and as home chefs became more and more sophisticated, wanting to recreate the atmosphere of a restaurant kitchen in their own homes, stainless steel came into vogue for modern kitchens. First the appliances began to get shiny and now entire counters and backsplashes are fabricated out of stainless. There are many pros and cons to using stainless in a kitchen but the bottom line is that it looks cool.

Newer materials such as Corian and other virtually impenetrable composite surfaces are perfect for a modern kitchen. Available in a wide range of colors, the smooth texture can turn a kitchen counter into a linear sculpture. Laminates are another way to create shiny surfaces in a kitchen. Imagine a high-gloss paint over every surface of a kitchen but now imagine it easy to clean and warm to the touch; that's what a laminated kitchen can feel like. Laminates come in a wide range of colors, patterns, and gloss levels so the options are endless. A hi-sheen cherry red, covering every appliance, cabinet front, and backsplash can instantly turn a kitchen into a hot rod. Mix bold primary colored laminates with stainless and lots of industrial glass for a slick modern kitchen.

> A kitchen may look and feel like a racecar, especially when adorned in stainless steel and red lacquer, but it works more like a laboratory for design as well as culinary experiments.

< Clean, white, and stainless—this kitchen was designed with surgical precision. A repeating pattern of rectangles—in metal, glass, and wood—play off each other like a puzzle. Using stainless steel in a backsplash and on major appliances is a good way to utilize the pros and cons of the material: It looks cool and reflects light but doesn't get as much wear, tear, and fingerprints as clad countertops would suffer.

< Professional quality kitchen appliances are matched with industrial elements for a workable modern kitchen. A chrome pot rack, metal louvers, and drawers that resemble a file cabinet are the ultimate industrial accents for a sea-green kitchen that asks to be taken seriously.

For a peaceful resting place, keep clutter to a minimum and invest in a comfortable mattress. Add a touch of romance with freshly cut flowers and sheer fabrics.

WHAT MAKES THE PERFECT BEDROOM?

Apart from soft textiles and controlled lighting, a good mattress, and a pleasing color scheme, the only essential ingredient is a personal touch. A bedroom is a sanctuary, a private domain; where you begin and end the day. Unlike public areas in the home that should be amenable to several different family members and guests, the bedroom must please only the sleeper. Some may prefer a restful place to crawl into bed and others will want an energizing environment to wake up to. For the first, consider a clean, modern space that is sparsely furnished and designed in a palette of soothing blues and white, for the latter a bright space dripping with color and completed with art on the walls might be appropriate.

REPOSE · STYLE · SANCTUARY

Whether it is a 700-square-foot master suite or an attic dormer for a visiting guest, decorating a bedroom requires specific consideration of its inhabitants. Stylistically, the bedroom should be harmonious with the rest of the house but beyond that, it should be a form of personal expression. Fill your own bedroom with things that are meaningful and beautiful–heirloom furnishings, luxurious textures, family photographs, a favorite painting. Design a guest bedroom in the same way but take care to make it universally comforting and calming.

After that, the rest is simple: You will need to consider the bed and bedding, lighting and window treatments, patterns and textures. With the help of some highly regarded designers, this chapter will explore the various options for creating the perfect bedroom. From French country to contemporary, minimalism to eclecticism the bedrooms on the following pages have one thing in common—they are the perfect bedroom for those who inhabit them.

REPOSE The most important element of any bedroom is the bed, of course. It may seem like a simple task, but the search for the perfect bed can quickly resemble "The Princess and the Pea." Consider the type and style of the bed frame—platform, four-poster, upholstered headboard, etc.—and how it relates to the size and scale of the room. Then consider the mattress and bedding: the possibilities for both can feel endless. It is important to remember that these elements are not accessories but rather the heart and soul of the bedroom; choose quality furniture and bedding that looks and feels comfortable.

Kelly Wearstler, a Los Angeles-based designer who has several hotels in her repertoire, says that a comfortable mattress is the number one priority in designing a bedroom. "People go into the bedroom to sleep," says Wearstler, "so the mattress is the most crucial element; a pillow top mattress is a good choice because it's firm yet soft." Next, find a bed frame that works within the room. "Getting the bed six to eight inches off the floor," suggests Wearstler, "is a great way to make the room seem larger. When it's up on legs, you can see the light under the bed and the room feels more spacious." Other designers prefer a low platform bed with a headboard that blends into the wall, or in some case, acts as the wall (right). And a uniform, all-white palette allows the bed to blend into the design of the room, so it doesn't disrupt the serenity. Still others believe that the bed should be a room within the room, with ornate hangings or romantic, sheer enclosures.

Whatever your preference for a sleeping platform, the bed is the smartest place to start. From there, you can choose bedding and blankets that complement this central element and express your personal style. Whether it's simple, solid sheets and a straightforward duvet or a cabbage rose coverlet and shams, choose the most luxurious bedding that you can afford. It may seem simply cosmetic but the difference between 350 thread-count and a poly-blend bedding feels like night and day.

> This high four-poster bed with colonial detailing makes the room appear larger by lifting the bed up off the floor. The natural bedding is perfect for a guest room where you can't anticipate the preferred colors of your guests.

Clean, white, and contemporary, this low bed uses a partition wall for a headboard and takes advantage of the space with a glass storage ledge that holds photo frames and flowers. Accessorizing a bedroom doesn't mean you have to fill it with personal objects; a single bud vase with bright Gerber daisies and some current reading material will do just fine.

In a room full of curves, this painted brass bed seems to float romantically under the eaves. Match furnishings by their bases, complement side tables that stand on curved legs with chairs that have similarly skinny legs. Here placing the bed up against the window and a dresser just under the sloped ceiling emphasizes the architecture of the room.

^ A master bedroom in a historic plantation house combines
Japanese painted silk walls with a French bed and simple
linen drapes for a perfect calm but exotic eclectic look.

THE PERFECT ECLECTIC BEDROOM

Eclecticism (or combining elements from many different styles and periods) has been gaining momentum in the world of interior design. A century ago, it was fashionable to blend one or two harmonious styles — Chinese and Louis XV or Japanese with mid-century modern — but now the look of one room can span several centuries and continents and still feel harmonious. A blend of perfect details culled from far-reaching inspirations can work together for a sophisticated and unique bedroom.

ACCESSORIES Bedrooms are ideal rooms for the eclectic approach because they are havens for personal touches and favorite pieces. New York interior designer Thomas Jayne created the unexpectedly layered rooms, seen here in a historic house on an old Southern plantation. "A bedroom is very personality driven; some people need a very plain space and others need all their favorite things around them. I like to think of the bedroom as a sanctuary where you reward yourself with having something beautiful to look at every morning and every night, like a favorite painting or fresh flowers."

< This chinoiserie dressing table and box covered in the same painted silk was designed by New York designer Thomas Jayne.

LAYERING A careful layering of old and new, Eastern and Western, simple and elaborate is, in fact, Jayne's signature style—a look he calls, "Antiquarian Modernism." Jayne notes, "Most people have a variety of things from different periods, but it is the mixture of style, texture, and scale that make a room more interesting." Here the combination of exotic elements like the Japanese-inspired painted silk walls, the chinoiserie dressing mirror and a nineteenth-century French bed, are countered by solid linen drapes. In a combination of Asian elements and classic colonial style, every scrolling shape is matched by a linear counterpart. Even the textures and patterns are balanced—classic white lace bedding defies the hand-painted print on the walls; a Persian rug sits atop simple sea grass carpeting.

QUIET "We wanted a calm room with exotic elements," says Jayne but his other priority was to make the room as comfortable as possible for both sleeping and relaxing. "You have to consider a way to control the light, both daylight and electric light." Here there are lined linen drapes to cover the large windows and balcony doors as well as several task lamps for bedside reading or sitting in the chair. "Bedrooms should always have at least one comfortable chair, or two for conversations," recommends Jayne. A chubby, little tufted armchair is covered in blue silk with a Chinese pillow for an alternate seat for relaxing.

Jayne's final advice: "A bedroom should be quiet, either acoustically, visually, or both." This doesn't mean muted colors and serene curves but rather an overall harmonious design that allows for comfort and quietude. The bedrooms seen here are perfect examples of hushed design that doesn't skimp on style. In a color palette that is both warm and cool and a design that feels reserved and yet daring, this room is meant for relaxing.

"The house, like many, is a mixture of styles," says Jayne. "People with taste are able to make that work and though it may be difficult to go for it, it can be so much more artful and rewarding." Here an integrated combination of styles and patterns, each one richer than the next, makes for a sophisticated and interesting take on southern living.

< A mixed match of framed prints above the bed and a classic mid-century modern armchair add a sense of surprise in the room that allows the contrasting patterns to feel easy rather than forced. "Interesting bed covers and printed linens are lovely in a bedroom," says Jayne of the striped boys room from the same southern house. "This felt like a daring combination of different stripes with a printed chintz, but it seems to work," says Jayne.

< Floor-to-ceiling green and white toile hides the awkward angles of this dormer bedroom and creates a lush landscape for informal elegance.

⌄ A guest bedroom in Atlanta is furnished with antique mahogany and botanical prints matched with quilts and awning stripes for a classic Provencal look.

THE PERFECT FRENCH COUNTRY BEDROOM

French country style, or Provencal as it is sometimes called, is always so warmly welcomed because it practically represents another lifestyle and time period.

FABRICS Open-weave cottons, densely quilted blankets, small prints of pastel nosegays matched with ticking stripes and other faded floral patterns— all of these elements come together for a look that is homespun country but sophisticated European. It says countryside rather than just plain, country.

Many trimmed fabrics alongside hand-painted wood furniture and worn antique pieces that have nearly translucent finishes, whether they are newly worn or actually old, create a simple yet elegant look that translates beautifully in a bedroom. Here are two examples of French country style; one that takes toile and Provencal furnishings to the height of fashion and another that makes country quilting impart a sense of European elegance.

PATTERNS The common reputation of this style is that too much is never enough and the latest craze of shabby chic found people layering faded chintz, one upon another with botanical patterns and florals climbing up the walls. However, simple style and restraint can also work for a homespun country look. For a more extreme look, a floor-to-ceiling application of toile de juoy fabric combined in various different patterns and colors can work like a back-drop to set the scene for country antiques and precious details.

> Classic quilted florals in muted blues
> and beige combined with ticking
> stripes and painted wood are a
> recipe for French country casual.

TOILE The classic European open-weave cotton print can serve as the art or the interest in a room; it literally allows color to permeate a room in a French country palette. Also, toile covers a myriad of architectural sins; you can use it to mask awkward-angled ceilings and dormer rooms. It's also very budget-minded because it can go a long way.

Try using one print along with its reverse print for an easy match. It's very easy to combine toile patterns—it's like a patchwork.

THE PERFECT CONTEMPORARY BEDROOM

Many people believe that contemporary style has to be deconstructive or spare, leaving them with a cold feeling about a room that seems lifeless. In fact, contemporary style is just the opposite with a fresh, modern take on using texture and pattern with clean lines and a mixture of subtle homage to the past and antiquity. In the two rooms seen here, designer DD Allen of Pierce/Allen in New York has created sophisticated fields of color and texture that create a haven for relaxation and meditation.

BALANCE "I like the feeling of sleeping in a cocoon," says Allen. "A bedroom should not feel like you are sleeping with walls of sheetrock." With a deft hand for layering texture upon texture, Allen has created bedrooms that seem designed for resting. Practically, absent is the whirlwind of color and pattern that overtakes many styles and designs. Instead, the soft balance of a leaf-appliquéd bed cover sits on a textured platform bed in a marriage of natural beauty. The other elements in the room, from the leather club chairs to the silk and bamboo on the windows, emphasize this natural balance of forms and textures—one soft and elegant, the other strong and practical.

COLOR AND TEXTURE "Bedroom walls should have some density, whether its fabric, color or curtains," says Allen. She suggests using colored paper or some type of texture on the ceiling since so much time is spent looking up. "I love upholstered walls in a bedroom," she adds, "almost like you are treating the whole room as though you are dressing it like a bed." Here a symphony of gray, black and white—from damask stripes to satin to felt on the actual bed, create a bed of absolute softness and sleep inducing textures and tones.

^ A harmony of black, white and gray creates a serene sleeping space that makes shades of softness feel like a rainbow.

< A perfect blend of textures, this urban bedroom design creates a haven high above a city that invites relaxation.

THE PERFECT GUEST ROOM

"A guest bedroom is a unique design challenge because it must be comfortable for almost anyone," says Jeffry Weisman of FisherWeisman Design in San Francisco, "but it must also fit the house it is part of and reflect the taste and style of its owners." In the softly lit monochromatic bedroom seen here Weisman had to create an inviting room that matches neatly tailored, classic tastes. "A layered use of creams and whites is always a winning combination in a bedroom. Undoubtedly this soft collection of matelasse on the bedspread and simple pleated draperies in a range of cream and pale green would be calming and inviting for any guest.

COMFORT Designer Thomas Jayne has a long list of elements that should be included for the perfect guest room; from a TV/VCR to extra blankets, he has made a science out of making his guest comfortable. One of Jayne's must-haves for a guest room is element of fun that guests will remember long after their stay is over.

< This guest bedroom, designed by Jeffry Weisman, invites serenity amid a flood of sunlight.

HOW TO FEEL AT HOME: THE GUEST BEDROOM TOP TEN:

COURTESY OF DESIGNER THOMAS JAYNE

1. Extra blankets and odd pillows; providing layers is the best way to make sure that your guests are comfortable.

2. A medicine cabinet stocked with toiletries that people always forget; razors, toothpaste, shampoo (normal-sized bottles, not ones that you steal from a hotel).

3. A bottle of water next to the bed.

4. Some fruit or something to snack on.

5. Current periodicals.

6. Books specially chosen from your library that would be particularly interesting to your guest—perhaps guidebooks to the area.

7. A recent novel.

8. Good window blinds, black-out shades if necessary to keep the light out.

9. Small TV and VCR with some movies.

10. Some memorable element or something more fun like a beautiful watercolor or an antique chest of drawers. It doesn't have to be something precious, just memorable.

Extra seating, unexpected design elements, and a layer of bed coverings make this a stylish example of Thomas Jayne's perfect guest bedroom.

FUN "I always like doing a really fun guest room, a place that no one would have in their own house," says Jayne. Here he describes his creation (seen above), "I wanted it to be a fun, over-the-top interpretation of a fifteenth-century Renaissance bed." Customized bed hangings and a coverlet made from antique Chinese textiles are fitted with unexpected details: the feathered bouquets on the corners of the posts were fashioned from Jayne's old Mardi Gras costume and the inside ceiling of the canopy was done in fuchsia fabric to be seen when lying down. Lastly, Jayne suggests sleeping in your guest bedroom at least once to make sure that it contains all the comforts of the rest of your home.

LIGHTING   There seems to be a consensus about what makes a bedroom perfect: the perfect bed, a well-placed lamp, soft sheets, extra seating, and a wealth of texture, pattern or colors that call to mind quiet and rest. Of course, the bottom line is that you can never forget about creating a stylish sanctuary.

Here a muted palette highlights a master bedroom. Soft lighting warms the sage green, gray, and natural bamboo behind the bed. Clever design keeps all the elements neat and tidy for a relaxing atmosphere. Recessed lighting is a good way to complement the lines of perfect architecture; the same goes for recessed window blinds. The drapes are made from a muted gray-green silk that reflects the light and creates a soft wall that envelops the room.

> Not for the cluttered collector, a sleek modern bedroom can be the perfect place to find serenity and slip into a quiet sleep.

> "A cushy upholstered headboard, delicious sheets, and perfect pillows make the room yours and lure you in," says Jeffry Weisman of this perfect bedroom—his own.

< A built-in headboard that also serves as an illuminated ledge, luxurious drapes, and a well-designed lighting scheme are the winning elements of this modern, muted bedroom.

This innovated padded-wall design behind the bed is a modern take on the classic headboard. Now that more and more platform beds are dropping their head and footboards, we find ourselves without any support. Building the headboard into the architecture of the room is a thoughtful way to create the comfort of support without sacrificing minimalist design. This version houses an illuminated ledge that makes the perfect stage for colored glass vases and artwork.

Simplicity reigns in this modern, streamlined bathroom. Large tiles make the room appear larger and the half wall provides just enough separation between toilet and bathtub—creating a perfect place to escape and relax after a long day.

WHAT MAKES THE PERFECT BATHROOM?

A perfect bathroom needs to walk a fine line between technology and pleasure.
Essentially it needs to be supremely functional as well as a pleasurable space to spend
time in. You may prefer a more utilitarian approach or crave a calm and contemplative
space—somewhere you can unwind and wash away the stresses of a hectic working
day. Whatever your wants and needs are, first and foremost ensure that your bathing
space reflects you and the life you lead within your home.

BALANCE · PROPORTION · COLOR · LIGHT

To obtain the perfect bathroom you will need to be conscious of the importance of proportion
and balance. This particular room demands the presence of certain fixtures and fittings, there's
simply no getting away from the need for a sink, toilet, or either a shower or bathtub. These
pieces will quickly fill up the available space, and your bathroom will need to be furnished and
decorated with pieces that are not only complementary to each other but also to the room as a
whole. Don't fear, though, for if you are working within a small space, for there are plenty of simple yet effective designer tricks that can be employed to give the impression of space and light.

Most importantly, however, don't forget that creating "the perfect bathroom" will only be
achieved if the relevant practical bones are in place—those that ensure smooth functionality.
Choosing your surfaces and fittings is an important job and you should ensure that they are
resistant to water, hardwearing, and importantly of course, beautiful to boot.

ANCE AND
OPORTION

Because we generally carry out several tasks in a bathroom we actually need quite a number of fixtures and fittings. These all need to visually sit comfortably side by side as well as physically within the confines of our particular internal space.

Consider a visit to salvage yards to source reclaimed pieces (a wonderful option) taking photos and measurements with you of any existing fixtures you have that you wish to work around. This will ensure that you find a suitable mate. Older pieces tend to be a lot larger, so bear that in mind as a small bathroom can easily be proportionally overwhelmed by these chunky pieces of the past. Remember that if you have decided to source and use, or retain period fittings, you will want part or all of your décor to reflect the same period.

< If you're going for an aged look, then keep all your fixtures to one particular era as much as is possible (or the illusion of an era if you are buying modern reproductions). See here how the pedestal basin and the towel rail sit in perfect harmony with each other—both alluding to a time past.

Search for a range of fixtures to suit the size of your bathroom—there are many that are specially suited to small spaces. Consider hiding your cisterns behind walls so that the toilet doesn't intrude more than is necessary. Also consider a wall-mounted sink, the taps for which will generally be wall-mounted ensuring the basin doesn't intrude out into the room more than is necessary. Make sure however that you position these taps high enough on the wall so that they don't interfere with hand washing and the like. Also installing a corner sink can save on space.

> Keep a look balanced by picking out a common feature and repeating it as has been done here with the blocky wood detailing. Both the bath and the basin have been raised on pedestals adding to the sense of balance and harmony.

< This bathroom unashamedly—and successfully—milks the nostalgic theme. Notice the unity of fixtures and fittings—the roll top bath, the traditional light fittings, the wallpaper, curtains, and the chair. They all fit into the same era. Be brave and bold when you are creating a look such as this.

Although small, this bathroom gives the impression of space without a traditional window. The clever use of skylights keeps the room light and airy.

THE PERFECT CONTEMPORARY BATHROOM

This simple yet effective bathroom has been cleverly designed with both genders in mind. It has struck that wonderful middle ground, which enables both men and women to feel comfortable there—so often not the case.

COLOR The soothing beige of the stone combined with the crisp white walls and ceiling has created a neutral piece of calm here. Notice how the shower screen, which is made out of toughened glass, has subtly added a welcome splash of color. This color has then been cleverly balanced out with the toothbrush holder on the shelf. Note also how the chrome finish of the taps ties in with the contemporary chrome radiator, ensuring uniformity and balance.

FLOORING Observe the large size of the stone tiles. In a small space, large tiles such as these will make a room appear significantly more spacious. Conversely small tiles, particularly on the floor will make the room feel smaller. Carrying these tiles up the wall and into the shower recess helps also to visually enlarge the space. Having a defined wall/ceiling line will only serve to reiterate the exact size of the floor area, which in this case is pretty small.

FURNITURE Taking the beige stone back up behind the toilet and sink has created a contrast of colors and therefore made an attraction out of the ceramic ware. A false wall has been created that serves several purposes: It hides the cistern as well as any unattractive plumbing; it provides a practical and well-proportioned shelf; and it creates a neat space for the cupboard to tuck into. Had the cupboard been left floating above an exposed cistern, it would have looked clumsy rather than streamlined. This false wall has also been extended through into the shower providing again a well-proportioned shelf, negating the need for wall-mounted soap dishes. Again simplicity reigns. The radiator has been added as a real feature, and with minimal intrusion and maximum design kudos it both heats and provides a designer towel rail.

SYMMETRY The shower wall and the two skylights at once define the symmetrical nature of this bathroom. Strong, straight lines—both horizontal and vertical—are the bones from which this bathroom builds it skeleton. Cleverly, though, the round mirror is an amusing departure from these angular lines, and coupled with the smooth curves of the basin and toilet, ensures that the entire room has been softened and beautifully saved from the clutches of clinical minimalism.

COLOR   When we think bathroom, what generally springs to mind is a room bathed in white, perhaps a splash
of color here and there. While in the past we went through an avocado and peach period with our
basins, baths, and toilets, we tend to revert to the age-old classic, ever-refreshing white, and rightly
so. Its association with crisp cleanliness (think starched nurses' uniforms) means it is always in
harmony with the idea of a bathroom. If you do want to add color, a successful and simple way to
do this is in details; tiles, shower curtains, and accessories such as soap dishes, vases, and towels.

Swimming pool-blue mosaic tiles have become very popular in bathrooms over recent years.
Evoke memories of childhood swims at municipal pools; the association with water is very strong.
Blue is also one of the cool colors of the spectrum and doesn't advance in a room, rather it recedes.
You will be left with a sense of space rather than oppression.

Highlight stunning bathroom fixtures, as seen here.
Draw attention to their organic shapes and their
gleaming bright white finish by painting the walls a
creamy color. Try combining cream and white for an
elegant yet subtle effect that will enable you to make
a focal point out of your ceramic ware.

Combine blue mosaics with bright white
to create a color combination that will sit
naturally and comfortably in your bathroom. Save on visual tedium by creating
tactile and textural interest using tiles of
varying sizes as has been done here.

Lift the tempo of your sharp white bathroom by choosing colored accessories. Here you can see how the addition of a small splash of color has broken up what could potentially have been a monotonous white space. You only need add the tiniest touches. Here, simply having green soap and a vase of pale yellow flowers has done a top job of dispersing the white without detracting from its crisp beauty.

Use color to set the tone of a bathroom. If the bathroom is to be used by all the family, males and females alike, then ensure its decoration shouldn't exclude or make either sex feel uncomfortable in there. All too often a bathroom will be created that is "girlie" and feminine and goes nowhere in helping male users to relax and enjoy being in there.

See how this room has used color in order to welcome either gender. Dark gray walls and accompanying dark gray details have created a strong and assured bathroom, softened with flowers and satin trimmed towels ensuring it is comfortable to women as well as men.

HOW TO GET THE LOOK: SLEEK GLASS

Glass has become a highly popular material in today's contemporary bathrooms. It is impermeable to water, strong, can be transparent or opaque (private or not), and it enables subtle divisions in the bathroom without impacting on space or light. Ever attractive, this material has become today's darling of the bathroom materials.

Defining Wet Areas The use of glass to define a shower space is particularly practical and attractive in this role. It can separate the shower from the rest of the room without diminishing the room's proportions, which will often happen if a solid, nontransparent material had been employed instead. Glass can now be molded into virtually any shape we choose, and paying a visit to a glass specialist will pay high dividends for anyone seeking to employ its benefits in their bathroom.

Adding Light If you need privacy but don't want blinds, which take away daytime light, then think about replacing the clear glass with frosted glass or tinted glass. Tinted glass is a simple way to add color and interest to your bathroom as well.

< Try tinting your windows as has been done here to great visual effect. The glass accessories have beautifully balanced the royal blue of the windows looking out. Not only do the windows provide visual interest though; they also ensure a level of privacy from the outside, which would have been unattainable from clear glass windows.

˅ This small bathroom makes perfect use of the clear nature of glass. The shower separation the glass provides is barely discernible and ensures that light can still flood in. If this were a solid nontransparent wall, this space would be far more claustrophobic, and the leafy view would certainly be obscured from sink users.

<Employ strong task lighting alongside or above your bathroom mirror. This will invariably be where you are applying make-up or shaving. Fluorescent lighting, while strong and suitable in this situation, can be somewhat harsh, so diffuse it behind a shade, as has been done here with frosted cylinders.

LIGHT   In the bathroom both artificial and natural light are key elements of good design. Often people don't realize just how much time designers put into planning lighting systems for a bathroom. It is often the feature that lifts one bathroom above the rest in design terms and should be thoroughly considered. Because you undertake a range of things in the bathroom from a long relaxing soak to quick rinsings to a lengthy make-up application session, you are advised to have at least two types of artificial lighting.

The mirror that will invariably be found above the sink needs to be well lit for this is where tasks such as make-up application and shaving take place. Consider strip lighting down the sides for even and strong task lighting. If not strip lighting, any form of lighting above or beside the sink top mirror will be distinctly better than nothing.

Often because bathrooms have tended to be tucked into small unlikely spots they have low ceilings. Because you are flinging your arms around while drying yourself it is a good idea to employ down lights that sit flush with the ceiling. These lights won't impinge on the limited space.

Natural light maketh the space, and in a bathroom—the most private of spaces in the home—often you'll be faced with the conundrum between wanting to achieve more privacy while at the same time improving the availability of natural light. Ponder several options, such as skylights, high-level windows, glass bricks, and frosted glass, for instance, before assuming that natural light isn't available.

Consider using a solid pane of frosted glass to enclose a shower/bathing space. It enables light to diffuse into the area, defines and confines the watery area, and also provides a suitable level of privacy should you be sharing the bathroom with other members of the family.

Try thinking laterally when attempting to preserve privacy yet still drawing natural light into the bathroom. Put some ceiling height windows in if possible. These will ensure that you retain your decorum while achieving the desired aim of more natural light and even peeps of the external lush nature.

Trick the eye into believing that your outdoor space is truly a seamless extension of your indoor space by mirroring the furniture that is used inside with the furniture used outside. Here it is identical, resulting in an optical illusion. The floor-to-ceiling window is also significant in creating this illusion, as (if kept clean) it dupes the eye into seeing simply one internal/external space.

WHAT MAKES THE PERFECT OUTDOOR ROOM?

A perfect outdoor room needs to satisfy man's inherent desire to commune with nature. Innate and unrealized, it is precisely this desire and its consequent satisfaction that makes us feel healthy and whole. In this book we have taken the liberty of defining outdoor rooms rather loosely—areas that may or may not be covered and may be either inside, outside, or somewhere in between. Take whatever is available in terms of nature, light, and sun and to use it in your own way to bring the outdoors in and take the indoors out.

SCALE · TRANSITION · LIGHT

The perfect outdoor room, no matter what type, somehow needs to break down these internal and external barriers—it needs to blur those boundaries and provide quirky transitions. When this is done successfully you will have achieved many things; you will have the feeling of both increased and more accessible outside and inside space.

What you need to do is to bring nature into your life on an everyday level. In our busy lives we don't always have time to go out and seek it. And remember that you don't have to have a large and lush garden to do this either—a small balcony can suffice—it can enhance your quality of life no end. Let us, with the help of insider information help you create the perfect outdoor room.

< Take note of how this tranquil and somewhat nautical setting has been cleverly landscaped to maximize the view. The plantings immediately draw your eye to the marina scene, and the well-proportioned chair has been perfectly placed so pensive daydreamers can lie back and enjoy this calming and peaceful environment.

SCALE Often when we think of creating or redefining an outdoor space so that it is integrated into our home in a successful and useful way, we don't consider proportion and balance issues. We think these are simply for our indoor areas. But the truth is that only by applying the same design principles to our outdoor rooms will we end up with a well-designed space, which is both useful and beautiful. We need our outdoor furnishings to be appropriate and well proportioned with regard to the space we are filling, and we need focal points and areas of intrigue just as we do in an interior room. These focal points will captivate the onlooker and could be anything—natural or unnatural—a view or perhaps a piece of sculpture, a bold piece of planting, or a funky piece of furniture.

< Frame views and you will be provided with what will seem like a constantly evolving painting. Note how this sheltered yet sunny spot literally frames the view and turns it into a powerful and absorbing focal point. Sometimes seeing less of something makes you more aware of it its beauty.

< The strong proportions of the old trees virtually cocoon you in this beautiful setting, and they can be perfectly appreciated, along with the distant water, from this raised vantage point. The two matching chairs set side-by-side in the sun provide the perfect platform for two people to sit and enjoy the vista.

Use a terrace or balcony to emphasize the merging of indoors and outdoors—have it create a neutral space, somewhere you can appreciate the benefits and comforts of the indoors with the beauty and scale of the outdoors.

Use pots and vessels to add intrigue and scale to the garden and you will see them immediately add a sense of style. Potted plants can be very helpful in ensuring that the proportion and balance of an area works well. Use large vessels filled with appropriate sized plants for large spaces and small for small. Move them around—see where they visually sit well.

MATERIALS Outdoor furniture comes in many guises and as such can be as grandiose or as simple as you wish. If it is to be exposed to the elements, however, you will need to ensure that it is either a material that can withstand the exposure or ensure that it can be easily moved inside out of the weather. For this reason, as well as for obvious aesthetic benefits, metal and wood are popular outdoor furniture materials. Wood is such a warm and elemental material—it sometimes looks as if it has just grown there. Both of these materials can be softened with cushions and the like if you want to create a more cozy and inviting seating arrangement. And, do be sure that the style and scale of your furniture suits its role and the environment you are placing it in.

Let furniture take the lead when defining what type of role you want your outdoor space to play. Here wicker furniture coupled with soft and comfortable cushions have created an inviting and cozy-looking living space. When using soft furnishings ensure that they are detachable and can be brought inside in inclement weather.

^ Ensure that your outdoor furniture suits the environment that it sits in. See how this rustic wooden furniture blends seamlessly into its environment and looks as though it was always meant to be.

Try creating a pocket of intimacy in your garden if you have a large, somewhat undefined space to play with. Here at the bottom of this rugged, seaside garden a reflective space has been created using furniture and potted plants to create a sense of place to reflect or hold private conversations while communing with nature.

SPACE   What is truly wonderful about an outdoor room is the enhanced space it can provide you and your family. The way we define space in our domestic environments has changed significantly over recent years. Where the indoors and outdoors used to be two completely distinct areas, there is now far more merging of the two. Where the outdoors used to be essentially concerned with plants and gardening, this is not so anymore. While we still want that connection to nature, we have taken that one step further and begun to look more laterally at areas and the ways in which we can use them and enjoy nature at the same time. Follow our design guidelines and you will be able to both physically and visually provide more room in your home.

> Define areas in your garden by raising areas and applying different underfoot surfaces. Here two separate areas have been defined and created in an urban garden setting. The potted plants and chairs on the raised platform have created a lovely little spot for a *tête à tête*. A second small area has been paved and furnished with two chairs positioned to catch the late evening sun.

Creating a usable outdoor room is simple if you focus spatially on the activity area. Set up a spot for relaxing, or maybe you'd rather tailor a space towards socializing, dining, or even sleeping. Ensuring that the inside and outside flow into and out of each other with a strong sense of unity will enable that one activity blends into another. If you have a large garden, try to create smaller more intimate spaces within it, give it some human scale from which to enjoy and marvel at the larger picture.

< No matter what style your home is, you can create a conservatory-style outdoor room and enhance your feeling of space. Do, however, try to keep your extension within the style of the house or it will look awkward and out of place. Here a sunny glass fronted and sided porch has been added harmoniously on to a log cabin creating a woody and warm outdoor room.

LIGHT

Natural light has much to do with the way we use our outdoor rooms, and we need to consider it carefully before laying out any areas in our gardens or as extensions of our homes. When creating an area that provides a transition from inside to outside think about using light and shade to blend them together harmoniously. And remember if you want to continue enjoying your outdoor space long after the sun has gone down then artificial lighting should also be a key consideration.

Using glass is of course a very popular way of providing a seamless indoor/outdoor transition as well as enabling us to be completely aware of the weather without necessarily needing to be out in it. In large conservatory style rooms we become very aware of the sun and the weather and we are able to enjoy its intricacies—dappled light, driving rain, indirect light, autumn light, strong blustery winds—they all create vastly different atmospheres, each with its own beauty.

See how a lighting system has lifted this under veranda space into a truly inviting and cozy area, as an alternative to the other unlit outdoor space in the background, which, in turn has completely lost its appeal with a lack of light. Do make use of candles in an outdoor setting, as the gentle flicker is beguiling and well suited to communing with nature. You will need to ensure that they are placed within a glass lantern or some such vessel as has been done here, so that the wind doesn't blow them out.

Try flinging your windows wide open and letting the sun and fresh air enter unabated. Quite simply this is all it sometimes takes to create a room with a perfect sense of the outdoors.

WHAT MAKES A PERFECT

If we were to make a list of the ten greatest interior decorators of the twentieth century, where would we begin? At the beginning, perhaps, with writer Edith Wharton and architect Ogden Codman, whose 1897 book *The Decoration of Houses* sounded the death knell for late-Victorian clutter and excess. But while the book was hugely influential, Wharton went on to write novels, and very few Americans ever saw Codman's decorating work.

INVENTIVE · PIONEERING · EXPERIMENTAL · LASTING

We could list some household names of fame—Ludwig Mies van der Rohe, Dorothy Draper, Andy Warhol—in hopes of conveying the vastness of the range of twentieth century design. But such a list is as unsatisfying as a strictly chronological one. How many Warhol rooms are there? What do they look like?

The decorators who created rooms we see as "perfect" weren't always the ones who started a trend: Wharton and Codman advocated it, but Elsie de Wolfe was the one who created beautiful and influential interiors in what she called her "old French look." The all-white room was much bruited about in European design circles. Charles Rennie Macintosh did it in 1903, Elsie de Wolfe and Oliver Messel worked towards it. But Syrie Maugham's theatrical midnight presentation of her newly decorated London house made the all-white room hers forever. A true trend-setter, she expressed the hard-edged modernity that would soon sweep aside historically informed decorating. The most important decorators of the twentieth century went beyond simply introducing a new idea; their work embodied the bigger changes of their times.

Thus, while Mies van der Rohe and Le Corbusier were pioneers of modernism, Jean-Michel Frank made pared-down rooms livable with rich materials and wit. Chintz was the fabric of choice for newly soft and feminine interiors, but Nancy Lancaster knew that it wasn't really pretty until it was old enough to be faded.

What makes a room perfect will always change with the times, but these ten decorators defined the concept in the first place.

Regina Cole

Billy Baldwin's signature slipper chair and sofa are upholstered in cotton printed to match the Matisse hanging placed above them. White walls, a white plaster lamp, crisp shapes and colors in the carpet and tables create a room that's modern, simple, and luxurious.

BILLY BALDWIN · 1903 – 1983
AMERICA'S FATHER OF MODERN DECORATING

Billy Baldwin swept out ostentation, jumble and clutter, and created a clean, modern sensibility for American rooms. He abhorred the florid, baroque, or rococo; always, his look was polished, snappy, and neat. His signature piece—the slipper chair—hugs the ground and wall, keeping his rooms uncluttered. Too many naked chair legs make a room look restless, he said. Furniture in his rooms was comfortable and streamlined, usually upholstered straight to the floor.

In the 1950s Billy Baldwin influenced Americans to leave their floorboards bare and to paint their walls white as a backdrop for modern furniture and antiques. He continued to favor plain walls, often in a glossy brown that became a trademark color. "Color should not be subject to the rules of fashion," he declared.

America's most popular 1960s decorator championed mixtures of periods and styles. The most important element in an interior, he said, was evidence of the inhabitant's personality.

WHAT MAKES IT PERFECT?
MODERN · STREAMLINED

Billy Baldwin achieved America's first truly modern rooms with equal emphasis on quality and on streamlined comfort.

DAVID HICKS · 1929 – 1998
REINVENTING ENGLISH TASTE FOR ROCK "N" ROYALTY

David Hicks was a true Englishman: He believed in the transforming power of fabric. His use of color and pattern was decidedly modern; he took the faded chintz out of English houses and brought in streamlined, modern decorating schemes. Rooms all over the world have escaped banality and snapped into focus with his signature piece, a geometrically patterned carpet. Even awkward rooms and dull furniture, David Hicks asserted, could be changed for the better through the use of the right pattern on the floor, lively upholstery fabric, or draperies.

David Hicks, who may have been the first "superstar" decorator with a client roster that included the English royal family and the Rolling Stones, used bold blocks of plain color to emphasize the architecture of a room. He liked coffee-brown walls, white upholstery and draperies, beiges, gunmetal, and splashes of hot pinks and oranges. Trademark are his "tablescapes," objects composed into artistic groupings.

At the height of his fame, David Hicks-designed products sold all over the world. Few decorators ever achieved such a high profile or exercised so much control: He scripted every detail of his own funeral, down to the fabric that lined the coffin.

WHAT MAKES IT PERFECT?
COLOR · PATTERN

Bold color, combined with "controlled clutter" on tabletops and walls and strong pattern underfoot is a modern way to emphasize the architecture of a room.

A geometrically patterned carpet, bold, precise use of coffee brown and hot pink, compositions of tabletop objects, and dramatic lighting are the key elements in this signature David Hicks-designed room.

In Mrs. Frick's New York bedroom, Elsie de Wolfe created a feminine environment she promoted as "The Old French Look." Key elements are the pale colors, tarnished gilding, floral and striped damask, and fresh flowers.

PERFECT LEGEND: ELSIE DE WOLFE · 1865 – 1950
AMERICA'S FIRST PROFESSIONAL DECORATOR

The feminine, refined style Elsie de Wolfe championed is still in our design vocabulary with glazed floral fabric, tarnished gilding, tender colors such as light grays, rose pink, soft blues, garden rooms, and the continuing reinvention of eighteenth-century art and design. Her maxim was "simplicity, suitability, and proportion" and her emphasis was on overall effects of elegance, light, and grace.

Elsie de Wolfe elevated the decoration of houses to the stature of a profession. Her wildly successful career began when, at age 40, she decorated the Colony Club, New York's first exclusive women's club. Instead of patterning them after the dark wood-and-leather rooms of men's clubs, she created interiors that evoked the pastoral fantasies of Marie Antoinette. Commissions from club members (her society friends) followed, and articles and books spread her influence beyond her rarefied circle, most notably in the 1913 book *The House in Good Taste*, serialized in *Ladies' Home Journal*.

She brought in light and swept Victorian clutter out of American homes, pioneered the trellised room as indoor garden pavilion, invented cove lighting, and began the practice of the decorator being paid a commission on purchases for the client. Although she loved and often used important French furniture, most notably in the decoration of the Stanford White designed Frick Mansion on Fifth Avenue, de Wolfe's emphasis was usually on an overall composition of decorative simplicity.

WHAT MAKES IT PERFECT?
LIGHT · FEMININE

Elsie de Wolfe's rooms expressed lightness and refined femininity in a classic idiom as an alternative to Victorian clutter and darkness.

JEAN-MICHEL FRANK · 1895 – 1941
THE LAST OF THE GREAT FRENCH FURNITURE MAKERS

A beige palette, walls lined with alternating squares of material, the Parsons table, a sofa in the shape of lips: The innovations of Jean-Michel Frank were adopted so enthusiastically that many became decorating clichés. But when this master of surrealism did his most influential work in the 1930s, he was seen as an uncompromising modernist whose designs were more brilliant than livable.

Jean-Michel Frank, part of the French avant-garde between the World Wars, had a master craftsman's reverence for materials. Famous rooms of the time held furniture upholstered in white leather, walls covered with alternating squares of white vellum, bronze doors inlaid with ivory, sharkskin cabinets, fireplace surrounds built of precious stone. In the United States, he designed brawny, rectilinear furniture for the modern interiors of captains of industry.

Though his life was tragic and brief, Jean-Michel Frank was, to many, the greatest decorator of the twentieth century, an artist who helped invent modernism while holding fast to an ancient tradition of quality.

WHAT MAKES IT PERFECT?
PARED · MATERIALS

Jean-Michel Frank's streamlined, expensively elegant interiors were at the vanguard of a new twentieth-century aesthetic. He experimented with rare materials and new forms in the context of painstaking craftsmanship.

An oak-veneer bedroom shows off signature touches—
an understated palette expressed in luxurious materials.
The coffee table is made of mica; the screen, chest of
drawers, and mirror are covered in straw marquetry.

John Fowler's aesthetic of "humble elegance" is expressed in this room's draped and swaged window treatment, paired chairs and sconces, chintz-upholstered sofa, and soft colors.

JOHN FOWLER · 1906 – 1977
THE GENIUS OF DRAPERIES

No one did fabrics like John Fowler. His beautifully designed and constructed draperies, especially, helped define the "English Country" look, developed during the 1940s and never out of style since then. Composed of colorful chintz, paired pieces of simple furniture, swaged and draped windows, and groups of pictures hung with ribbons and bows, the style has a refined charm descended both from Regency interiors and country cottages.

Fowler preferred cream ware to porcelain, color and pattern to plain white, and his ideals of beauty were found in old farmhouses and in eighteenth-century French furniture. He liked to sprinkle his very English rooms with pieces of French furniture, usually chairs, for lightness and elegance.

He came to interior design from work as an artisan. From the start, he was drawn to textiles; many of his designs were inspired by collected scraps of eighteenth and early nineteenth century fabric. John Fowler's style reached its zenith while working with the lively American expatriate Nancy Lancaster, whose aunt, Lady Astor, called them "the unhappiest unmarried couple in England." In retirement, he became England's greatest restorer of National Trust houses.

WHAT MAKES IT PERFECT?
ENGLISH COUNTRY · ELEGANCE

John Fowler's rooms are comfortable and elegant without being grand or stiff with soft colors, simple forms, and country charm.

MADELEINE CASTAING · 1895 – 1992
THE DOYENNE OF PARISIAN DECORATORS

There's a kind of room that is so very French: dark, dramatic, furnished with early nineteenth century furniture, eclectic lighting fixtures, carefully chosen curios, and small, exquisite chairs. It is such a characteristically French combination of lightness, drama, and formality that it still surprises us to know that it was created in the middle of the twentieth century.

Madeleine Castaing opened her antiquarian shop in Paris during the gray days of World War II, and residents of the occupied city stood at the windows and drank in the nostalgia she provided. Her highly personal style varied very little over the next fifty years. She loved Empire and Directoire furniture, mid-nineteenth century glass lamps, the use of black, and her signature blue-green. She was among the first to mix furniture from different periods, and to place antiques into modern rooms.

Both decorator and antiquarian, Madeleine Castaing's position and influence in France was like that of John Fowler's in England: she developed a décor that combined modern lightness and scale with an idealized view of France's past.

WHAT MAKES IT PERFECT?

DRAMATIC · STYLE MIX

In her highly personal, eclectic blendings, Castaing achieved a balance of elegance, grace, and intensity, the essence of French period decorating.

Madeleine Castaing's salon or games room expresses Gallic nostalgia and wit with the artful use of deep color, Empire furniture, small tables, and eccentric nineteenth-century lighting fixtures.

Warm, saturated colors, beautiful proportions,
and comfortable seating in a classical idiom
evoke lost grandeur in this London room Nancy
Lancaster designed for herself.

NANCY LANCASTER · 1897 – 1994
HAUTE DÉCOR IN HIGH SOCIETY

When she married into the English landed gentry, Nancy Lancaster found their country houses to be damp, drafty, filled with Victorian clutter, and short on bathrooms. In her hands the country estates became comfortable and elegant. She installed bathrooms and radiators, swept out nineteenth-century mahogany and horsehair in favor of graceful eighteenth-century antiques, applied saturated colors to the walls, hung pictures at eye level, placed comfortable sofas and chairs close to the fireplace, arranged furniture into conversation groups, and knew how to create a flattering combination of warm colors and good lighting. Nancy Lancaster preferred softly faded chintz to new. She loved continuity, family history, and objects made meaningful by generations of use.

Though she had no formal training, this southern belle had a keen sense of a room's best purpose and an unfailing eye for proportion; her rooms are famous for their natural traffic flow and their unstudied coherence. Both her interiors and her gardens achieved luxurious informality within classic frameworks.

After World War II, Nancy Lancaster bought Lady Sibyl Colefax's London decorating firm, renaming it Colefax and Fowler. She and John Fowler were famous for their rows; together they created some of England's most beautiful interiors.

WHAT MAKES IT PERFECT?
COMFORTABLE · CLASSIC

Nancy Lancaster combined a deep reverence for old family homes with a modern appreciation for function and physical comfort.

SISTER PARISH · 1910 – 1994
THE BIRTH OF AMERICAN HIGH STYLE

If you have an American quilt, a painted floor, or rag rugs, blame Sister Parish. She was the powerhouse decorator who, for six decades, defined the look we now associate with old money. Part faded-elegance, part understated-opulence, it is composed of comfortable furniture, family heirlooms, needle pointed pillows, animal portraits, flashes of daring color, and lots of chintz.

Sister Parish rose to national prominence in 1961, when she applied this highly personal decorative style to the White House's family quarters for the Kennedy family. By then, she had been refining it for thirty years. Born into the upper class, Sister (a brother's childhood nickname) Parish went to work when her husband's income fell during the Depression. Her style was informed by her own taste and experience, not by academic training. Her peers remarked that she simply "felt" her way along while decorating, and she claimed to be hopeless with a scale ruler. Perhaps it was this unstudied approach that gave her interiors their fresh, unselfconscious beauty.

WHAT MAKES IT PERFECT?
OPULENT · HEIRLOOMS

Sister Parish stressed comfort, family, flowers, and refined a look that seemed to have evolved naturally. She was the first American decorator to use handcrafted materials in high-style interiors, which started a national craze for quilts and rag rugs.

^ A room designed by Sister Parish never looked terribly new, even if it was. She achieved the effect with an artful mixture of flowered fabric, needlepoint, family pieces, and portraits of animals.

Syrie Maugham's decorating was all about drama:
white walls, pickled Georgian furniture, and
neo-baroque grandeur in a stripped-down,
modern style are signatures in one of her rooms.

SYRIE MAUGHAM · 1879 – 1955
THE ALL-WHITE ROOM

Although the concept was in the air, Syrie Maugham was the "smart young thing" who became forever associated with the all-white room. In April of 1927 she invited her artistic friends, and at midnight threw open the doors to her newly decorated seventeenth-century house in King's Road, Chelsea. It was a wonder of white, including pale beige satin sofas, low, horizontal silver tables, a mirrored screen, and "pickled" Georgian chairs. The 1930s were the first time it became more fashionable to decorate according to new, modern precepts instead of historic styles, and Syrie Maugham lead the way. Her passion for pickling set up a decorating craze, to the distress of traditionalists. Many a patinated piece of old furniture was stripped, bleached, limed, and waxed for the fashionable pale finish.

Syrie Maugham herself only decorated one all-white room, her own; later commissions incorporated first blue, then red, then myriad's of color. But she was known as the princess of pale forever: When she traveled to India with Elsie de Wolfe in the late 1930s, a friend quipped it was "to paint the Black Hole of Calcutta white."

WHAT MAKES IT PERFECT?

PALE · MODERN

Syrie Maugham expressed luxury in a modern, machine-age sensibility. Her most successful rooms were grand, elegant, pale, and dramatic.

T. H. ROBSJOHN-GIBBINGS · 1909 – 1973
A NEW CLASSICISM

While other American decorators vigorously socialized, London-born Terence Harold Robsjohn-Gibbings, trained in architecture and transplanted to the United States in 1936, visited museums and sketched the chairs depicted on ancient Greek vases. His rooms are classical in their cool, clean lines, blond wood furniture, and unadorned sensibility.

T. H. Robsjohn-Gibbings believed in the cause of modern design, but in a historical context. The Klismos chair, his version of an ancient form, was a signature piece in interiors that were uncluttered and spare, but saved from severity by the use of rich materials. He espoused modernism, but disliked what he saw as the lifeless utilitarianism of Ludwig Mies van der Rohe and Le Corbusier.

In 1944 Robsjohn-Gibbings ("Gibby" to his friends) published *Goodbye, Mr. Chippendale*, which made fun of the American passion for reproductions of Georgian furniture. The influential book advocated that Americans turn to Frank Lloyd Wright for furnishing inspiration, instead of George III or Louis XVI. T. H. Robsjohn-Gibbings alluded to the styles of the past without copying or pastiche, a unique feat in twentieth century interior design.

WHAT MAKES IT PERFECT?

PURE · RICH

Pure forms and rich materials made interiors and furniture designed by T. H. Robsjohn-Gibbings elegant and classic. While clearly modern, his designs were evocative of their ancient Greek influences.

^ "Gibby" was disdainful of what he called the cult of antiques and "bric-a-brac-o-mania." The ancient Greeks informed his furniture in simple, rich, and classic rooms.

PHOTO CREDITS

Abode/Trevor Richards, 59; 88; 90 (right); 92

Abode/Tim Imrie; 67 (bottom); 71 (bottom)

Courtesy of Laura Ashley, 18

Roland Beaufre/Top Agency, 123

Fernando Bengoechea/Franca Speranza s.r.l.,
    19; 21;107

Björg, 34; 35; 44; 45; 49; 50; 51; 52; 53; 63 (both);
    67 (top); 71 (top); 82; 83 (bottom); 84; 85; 93

Antoine Bootz, 33 (both); 36; 40; 42; 56; 76 (both)

Courtesy of Chambers, 77

Pierre Chanteau, 68; 69

Grey Crawford/Beate Works, 12

Courtesy of Editions du Regard, 119

English Heritage, 128

Feliciano Studio, 127

The Frick Collection, 116

Ken Hayden/Red Cover, 10; 11

Winfried Heinze/Red Cover, 25

Horst/©Vogue, Condé Nast Publications, Inc., 112; 124

John Kane/Austin Patterson Disston Architects, LLC
    65 (top)

David Duncan Livingston, 54; 55 (bottom); 57

Maura McEvoy/Thomas Jayne Studio, Inc.
    72;73;74;81

Keith Scott Morton, 55 (top); 60; 61; 62; 70

Maynard Parker, 131

Eric Roth/Anne Fitzgerald, Design 38

Jeremy Samuelson, 13 (both); 15; 22; 26; 27

James Shanks/Pierce/Allen Design, 78; 79

Tim Street-Porter/Beate Works, 28; 29; 37; 66

Tim Street-Porter/Fisher Weisman
    Design&Decoration, 41; 80; 83 (top)

Tim Street-Porter/BAM, 65 (bottom)

Andrew Twort/Red Cover, 17

Simon Upton/The Interior Archive, 43

Brian Vanden Brink, 39 (left); 102; 106

Brian Vanden Brink/Drysdale Associates, 58; 93 (left)

Brian Vanden Brink/Elliott & Elliott Architects, 86

Brian Vanden Brink/Quinn, Evans Architects, 87
    (bottom); 98 (bottom); 100

Brian Vanden Brink/Scholz & Barclay Architects,
    90(left); 99

Brian Vanden Brink/Weston & Hewitson Architects, 91

Brian Vanden Brink/Rob Whitten, Architect 94

Brian Vanden Brink/Scogin Elam and Bray
    Architects 95 (right)

Brian Vanden Brink/Weatherend Estate Furniture,
    98 (top)

Brian Vanden Brink/Centerbrook Architects, 101

Brian Vanden Brink/Mark Hutker Architects, 103 (top)

Brian Vanden Brink/Bullock & Co. Log Home
    Builders103 (bottom)

Brian Vanden Brink/Peter Rose Architect, 104 (left)

Brian Vanden Brink/Scott Simons Architect, 105

Fritz von der Schulenburg/The Interior Archive,
    115;120

Andreas von Einsiedel/Red Cover, 16; 24; 39
    (right);104 (right)

Paul Warchol/Michielli & Weytzner, Architects, 23

Paul Warchol/ Morris Sato Studio, 46; 47; 48

Paul Warchol/Marlys Hann, Architect, 96

Henry Wilson/The Interior Archive, 87 (top)

Vicente Wolf/Vicente Wolf Associates, 31 (both)

DIRECTORY OF DESIGNERS

Austin Patterson Disston Architects, LLC
376 Pequot Avenue
Southport, CT 06490
203-255-4031

Brian Murphy
BAM
150 West Channel Rd.
Santa Monica, CA 90502
310-459-0955

Lee Bierly
Bierly-Drake Design
17 Arlington St.
Boston, MA 02116
617-247-0081

Bullock & Co. Log Home Builders
176A Mill Street
Creemore, Ontario, Canada LOM 1G0
705-466-2505

Peter F. Carlson & Associates, LLC
162 Joshuatown Road
Lyme, CT 06371
860-434-3744

Centerbrook Architects,
67 Main Street
Centerbrook, CT 06409
860-767-0175

Chambers
P.O. Box 7841
San Francisco, CA 94120-7841
800-334-9790

Celeste Cooper
Repertoire
114 Boylston St.
Boston, MA 02116
617-426-3865

Drysdale Associates Interior Design
1733 Connecticut Ave NW
Washington, DC 20009
202-588-7519

Elliott & Elliott Architects
P.O. Box 318
Blue Hill, ME 04614
207-374-2566

Fisher Weisman Design & Decoration
616 Minna Street
San Francisco, CA 94103
415-255-2254

Michael Graves & Associates
341 Nassau Street
Princeton, NJ 08540
609-924-6409

Marlys Hann, Architect
52 West 84 Street
New York, NY 10024
212-787-1680

Mark Hutker & Associates Architects
Box 2347
Vineyard Haven, MA 02568
508-693-3344

Thomas Jayne Studio, Inc.
136 East 57th Street
New York, NY 02116
212-838-9080

Cheryl & Jeffrey Katz
60 K Street
Boston, MA 02127
617-464-0330

Michielli & Weytzner Architects
149 Accabonac Road
East Hampton, NY 11937
631-329-6148

Morris Sato Studio
219 East 12th Street
New York, NY 10003
212-228-2832

Michael Pierce & DD Allen
Pierce/Allen
80 Eighth Avenue
New York, NY 10011
212-627-5440

Jennifer Post
25 East 67 Street
New York, NY 10021
212-734-7994

Quinn, Evans Architects
1214 28th Street NW
Washington, DC 20007
202-298-6700

The Office of Peter Rose, Architect
1 Kendall Square
Building 1700
Cambridge, MA 02139
617-494-8115

Scholz & Barclay Architects
P.O. Box 1057
Camden, ME 04843
207-236-0777

Scogin Elam and Bray Architects
75 J.W. Dobbs Ave NE
Atlanta, GA 30303
404-525-6869

Scott Simons Architect
15 Franklin Street
Portland, ME 04101
207-772-4656

Kelly Wearstler
Kwid
317 North Kings Road
Los Angeles, CA 90048
323-951-7454

Weatherend Estate Furniture
6 Gordon Drive
Rockland, ME 04841
207-596-6483

Weston & Hewitson Architects
222 North Street
Hingham, MA 02043
781-749-8587

Rob Whitten, Architect
37 Silver Street
Box 404 DTS
Portland, ME 04112
207-774-0111

Vicente Wolf Associates
333 West 39th Street
New York, NY 10018
212-465-0590

ABOUT THE AUTHORS

SARAH LYNCH

Interior design writer and editor Sarah Lynch writes the monthly Colorways column for *Metropolitan Home* magazine, and she is the author of *Bold Colors for Modern Rooms* (Rockport 2001). Sarah Lynch wrote the chapters on Perfect Dining Rooms, Perfect Open Plan, Perfect Kitchens, and Perfect Bedrooms.

PIP NORRIS

With a career begun in travel writing and two books behind her in this genre, Pip Norris, on moving to London, made the switch to interior design writing, a subject she has long been passionate about. *The Perfect Room* is the second interior title Pip has co-authored, the first being *Untouched* for British publishers, Conran Octopus Limited. Pip Norris wrote the chapters on Perfect Out Door Rooms, Perfect Baths, and contributed to Perfect Living Rooms.

REGINA COLE

Regina Cole writes on architecture, interior design, and the history of the decorative arts. She is an editor at *Old-House Interiors* magazine, and she lectures on the subject of historic kitchen styles, with emphasis on their suitability for today's way of living. She lives in Gloucester, Massachusetts. Regina Cole wrote the Perfect Legends segment of the book.

DEDICATION

Special thanks to project manager Nora Greer for pulling together many pieces into a perfect whole; to editor Kristy Mulkern, for her dedication and gentle manner; to photo editor Betsy Gammons for finding the perfect room one hundred and twenty times; to Regina Cole for her speed and style in writing Perfect Legends of Design; to Gregor Cann, for last minute thoughts on perfection. Thanks, too, to editors Martha Wetherill and Shawna Mullen for the perfect book idea, and to Helen Thompson and Ann McArdle for the framework in "Perfect Living Rooms."

Grateful thanks to art directors Silke Braun and Regina Grenier for steering the design of the book to perfection.